TITAN

ONE MAN'S DREAM

DOUGLAS JOHN FAULKNER-WOOLLEY

HIS CLAIMS ON BRITAIN'S TWO MOST FAMOUS LINERS
(QE1 AND TITANIC)

A Biography

by

CLIVE AMPHLETT & D. J. FAULKNER-WOOLLEY
DIVING INFORMATION BY S. J. BILSBY

DOUGLAS JOHN
FAULKNER-WOOLLEY
ONE MAN'S DREAM

HIS CLAIMS ON BRITAIN'S TWO MOST FAMOUS LINERS (QE1 AND TITANIC)

This book is copyright of
CLIVE AMPHLETT
and
© DOUGLAS JOHN FAULKNER-WOOLLEY
1998
ISBN 0 9533175 0 1

Special Edition

All rights reserved
Published by
Seawise Publication
680 Green Lane
Ilford Essex (U.K.)

Designed & Printed By
Akshar Design & Print
656 Green Lane
Ilford Essex (U.K.)

HMV

This voucher can be exchanged at any HMV store in the United Kingdom and Republic of Ireland. It can be exchanged in part payment for goods totalling £5.00 or more until 24th December 1999. Only one 'Christmas 1999' voucher per purchase. Please note this voucher cannot be exchanged for cash.

HMV

Christmas 1999
Valid to 24th December 1999 on purchases
totalling £5.00 or more at HMV stores only.
Only one 'Christmas 1999' voucher per purchase

one pound

gift voucher

£1

one pound

CHAPTERS

ACKNOWLEDGEMENTS

TO PRESS REPORTERS:

Allan Douglas
Lena Anderfelot
Nicholas Holmes
Tony Elliot
Tony Bugay
Mike Truscott
Judson Bennett
John Hay
Colin Carr
Penny Hart
Michael Ford
Ron Tibbs
Nikki Radford

MEMBERS OF TEAM:

Stephen J. Bilsby
Charles H. Betts
William W. A. Bissett
Dennis R. Bissett
Dr. A. Balas.
P. Deacon
H. R. Carlon
P. Biggs
Rickey Grange
J. Copsey
A. Tang
**DOUGLAS JOHN
FAULKNER-WOOLLEY**

SPECIAL THANKS TO:

Lord Graham of Edmonton; London.
Senator Le Main
Ian Twinn MP
J. R. Bower
Mr. James Barker
Mr. J. Singh-Soor
Mr. N. Patel

also to Mr. Douglas Faulkner - Woolley's sisters, Mrs. Ann Copsey and Miss Hilda Hood and Douglas' brother-in law Mr. Michael Copsey, Mr. George Woolley, Thomas Woolley, Richard Amphlett, John Amphlett, E. F. Faulkner, F. Woolley and Alfred Chambers

Blackpool Evening Gazette
Liverpool Echo
Pravda (U.S.S.R.)
Now magazine
Paddington Murcurey
History of Ships (Part 52)
New English Library

South China Morning Post
Hong Kong Star
Southern Evening Echo
Shropshire Star
Jersey Evening Post
THE QUEEN OF TITANIC EXPEDITIONS

With gratitude to my
Most Trusted Friend
FLINT
1983-1997
For all time
MITIS DEPONE COLLA

LATE NEWS - STOP PRESS

THE CONAKRY STORY.

Press Cuttings

THE TITAIU.

The most remarkable prophecy ever made must surely be the story of the *Titanic*, the great ocean liner which sank on her maiden voyage in 1912 with terrible loss of life. In 1898 a novel by a struggling writer, Morgan Robertson, predicted the disaster with uncanny accuracy.

Robertson's story told of a 70,000-tonne vessel, the safest ocean liner in the world, which hit an iceberg in the Atlantic on her maiden voyage. She sank and most of her 2500 passengers were lost because, incredibly, the liner had only 24 lifeboats – less than half the number needed to save all the passengers and crew on board.

On 14 April, 1912, the real-life tragedy occurred as the 66,000-tonne *Titanic* was making her maiden voyage across the Atlantic. She, too, hit an iceberg; she, too, sank. And, like the liner in the novel, she did not have enough lifeboats – only 20, in fact – and there was terrible loss of life. Of the 2224 people on board the luxury liner, 1513 perished in the icy waters. Robertson even came close to getting the vessel's name right – he called it the SS *Titan*.

Another work of fiction about a similar tragedy had appeared in a London newspaper some years earlier. The editor was a distinguished journalist, W. T. Stead, who added a prophetic note to the end of the story: 'This is exactly what might take place, and what will take place, if liners are sent to sea short of boats.' By an ironic twist of fate, Stead was one of the passengers on the *Titanic* who died for that very reason.

In late 1971 Captain S Kingsley, a founder/ director of Salvors Ltd of Jersey, also O.T.S. of Portsmouth, was seized at gun point with eleven members of his crew that were on board the 620 ton vessel *Salvager*. At the time they were on their way to salvage a ship on the coast of Conakry, West Africa. We do not know why they were arrested - they were on their own ship, but the British Government did not take long to get them set free. As all the members of the crew had been arrested the *Salvager* was left to drift and was grounded at the mouth of the River Nunez.

Kingsley owned a company by the name of Shiptrail with a Mr Frank Tophan. They planned to salvage a German submarine off Penang that contained a fortune in mercury. The German Government sent in a gunboat to stop them.

Also in 1971, Kingsley was involved with a vessel called *Harry Sharman*, which was another of Kingsley's salvaging tugs. This, together with the *Salvager*, was sent to the Isle of Wight to salvage a vessel called *Pacific Glory* that was owned by Mr C.Y. Tung of Hong Kong - the same man who owned the former *QE1*. In the process of salvaging *Pacific Glory*, *Harry Sharman* ran aground and can still be seen there to this day at low tide and has also been seen by Doug, Steven and Flint (Doug's dog).

After the *Harry Sharman* ran aground it was raided in the dead of night. It was reported that they had taken brass fittings, several other parts and the cathode ray tube.

PREFACE   DMSJFFIC

This is a true account of my life and the events that led up to the
salvage contracts of the QE1 in Hong Kong and the RMS Titanic. This
book is about Douglas John Faulkner-Woolley, "the not so ordinary man".
I am most grateful for moral support received from the late Bill Lasson, Mr
Marcuss Rees MP of Llanelli (South Wales, Cymru) and the late Captain
Hutton of Scotland. "Doug" they said, "when you raise the cash, sir, go
ahead, however when you raise the QE1 the world will salute you".
"However always remember that your main contention will be from the
sharks, the kind that will take over your plans and projects as reported in
the press and TV.
In 1972 the Marine Court in Hong Kong gave the verdict that the fires on
the QE1 were started deliberately by person/s unknown and to date have
not been brought to trial.At the time it was decided that I would be allowed
to salvage the QE1 at a total cost of £40,000 (a small sum in todays terms)
and this too would be self financing from the sale of the fuel and the
Film/Media rights to the story. I have to date, been unable to see this contract through for various reasons which I have explained.
Finally I wish to thank John Faulkner Copsey, Clive Amphlett, R.J.
Amphlett-Grange, diving info by Steven J. Bilsby and the officers and staff
of the Supreme Court of Hong Kong and the Royal Court of Jersey, C.I.
My sincere thanks to all whose names I have not mentioned,without whose
help I would have been unable to complete this project. **D.J.F-W**

1

The three windows on the north side of the nave contain a few fragments of fine 14th-century stained glass worked up with modern glass. Of the Annunciation in the westernmost window the old portions are the head of our Lady and a part of her dress. The head of St. Elizabeth and a few other fragments in Visitation are old the Purification, is the border.

DOUGLAS JOHN FAULKNER-WOOLLEY

In the head of the east window are remains of heraldic glass with the arms of Mortimer, Despenser, Beauchamp and Dai

There is one be scription of the or upon it, and is as

THE NOT SO ORDINARY MAN

Hount 1668 . Soli Deo Gloria, Pax Hominibus. Below on a shield are the founder's initials, ' J.M.,' for John Martin.

The plate includes a cup of peculiar pattern, with hall mark 1812, the gift of Rev. R. H. Amphlett, 1816, and a silver paten with the inscription on the foot 'The humble gift of Ester Paul to Hadzor Church August 4 1816.'

The registers previous to 1812 are as follows : (i) all entries 1554 to 1746 ; (ii) baptisms and burials

1750 to 1812, marriages 1750 to 1754 ; (iii) marriages 1754 to 1812.

The advowson followed the descent ADVOWSON of the manor,[48] and now belongs to Major H. G. H. Galton. Although the church is known to have existed in 1268,[49] it is ... on of Pope Nicholas in ... Dissolution its value was ... ted an altar at Hadzor.[51]

An acre of meadow which had been given for the maintenance of lights in the church of Hadzor was ... e 16th century at 20d.[52] ... Amphlett, by his will late), gave to the poor the 3 6s. 8d. to remain as a certain stock for ever. No payment is now made in respect of this charity.

In 1745 Mrs. Mary Wood, by deed, conveyed to trustees 2 a. called Hempland upon trust out of the rents and profits to pay 20s. yearly to the poorest housekeepers, and the residue of the rents to the rector of the parish.

The land so charged is understood to be occupied by the rector for the time being, but the annuity is not now paid.

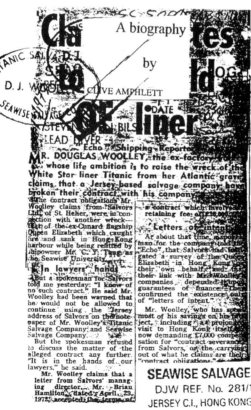

A biography by CLIVE AMPHLETT

...HN FAULKNER-WOOLLEY
...ITANIC Salvage Project
...d Seawise Salvage co.s
Jersey C.I.
...RITISH HONG KONG

MR. DOUGLAS WOOLLEY, the ex-factory whose life ambition is to raise the wreck of the White Star liner Titanic from her Atlantic grave claims that a Jersey-based salvage company have broken their contract with his company.

The contract obligations Mr. Woolley claims from Salvors Ltd. of St. Helier, were in connection with another wreck—that of the ex-Cunard flagship Queen Elizabeth which caught fire and sank in Hong Kong harbour while being refitted by shipowner Mr. C. Y. Tung at the Seawise University.

In lawyers' hands
But a spokesman for Salvors told me yesterday: "I know of no such contract." He said Mr. Woolley had been warned that he would not be allowed to continue using the Jersey address of Salvors on the notepaper of Mr. Woolley's Titanic Salvage Company and Seawise Salvage Company.

But the spokesman refused to discuss the matter of the alleged contract any further. "It is in the hands of our lawyers," he said.

Mr. Woolley claims that a letter from Salvors' managing director, Mr. Brian Hamilton, dated April 29, 1972, accepted the terms of

... a contract which involved retaining fees ...

Letters of intent
At about that time, a ... man for the company told the "Echo", that Salvors had ... gated a survey of the Queen Elizabeth in Hong Kong ... their own behalf, and that their link with Mr. Woolley's companies depended upon guarantees of finance ... confirmed the existence only of "letters of intent".

Mr. Woolley, who has sp... most of his savings on his pro... ject, including a projected visit to Hong Kong itself, now demanding £7,000 compensation for "contract severance" from Salvors, or the carrying out of what he claims are their "contract obligations."

SEAWISE SALVAGE CO.
DJW REF. No. 281/162
JERSEY C.I., HONG KONG, U.K.

PROLOGUE

We have written this book about Mr D.J. Woolley as he is quite unique-as far as it is possible for an ordinary person to be unique. He has the rights to two of the most famous British ships ever to have set sail. They are the Queen Elizabeth I and the Titanic.

The book is about how he first got interested in the Titanic, about two of his Great Aunts had booked passages on the ship but changed their minds at the last moment and also about how he became involved with the QE1.

For the last 20 years he has been fighting not one, but two Court cases, one in Jersey, C.I., the other in Hong Kong. To have a court case in any one of these places for 20 years would be difficult enough, but he has managed to keep them both in the courts and he has done all this without the aid of solicitors.

Mr. Douglas John Woolley back in the 1960's attained worldwide media coverage of his plans to raise the Titanic and the method he was going to use. It was at that time, that he was appealing for backers to come forward so as to carry out the final survey and prepare his team members in a one -chance bid to raise the Titanic.

In 1972 the former QE1 (now called Seawise University) was set alight and sank in Hong Kong harbour, surrounding mysterious doubt on the cause of the six fires that were started. Mr Woolley wrote to the owner and asked if he could salvage the QE1 as a test run for the Titanic. The owner, a Mr C. Y. Tung confirmed that he liked the idea and that he could go ahead with the salvage work.

Mr Woolley was then approached by some businessmen from Jersey. One of these businessmen was Mr S. Kingsley, who offered to carry out the contract on the QE1 for a part in the Titanic salvage.This was agreed, but they never carried out any work on the salvage - and that is what the two Court cases are about.

Although Mr Woolley is now starting to put the final plans together, it will not affect the Court cases, apart from the amount of money it will now cost to carry out the salvage.
In 1972 it would have cost £40,000 but now it will cost approximately £18 million. At the end of the project a complete bill will be submitted to the Courts for reimbursement from the people who made the original contract in 1972.

M.V. Lady Hobarthy about 120 years ago and White Star Atlantic in 1873 sank at approximately the same spot as the Titanic did in 1912.

FROM THE
OPPOSITION CHIEF WHIP

House of Lords
London   SW1A 0PW

Tel: 0171 219 3234

25 September 1995

<u>TO WHOM IT MAY CONCERN</u>

I have known Doug Woolley for more than twenty years, when he first
came to my attention as an employee of a firm in which my son worked.
First of all, I believe that Doug is absolutely sincere and convinced
of the rightness of the case that he espouses. From time to time, at
his request, I have been very happy to intercede with authorities both
legal and Governmental here, on the island of Jersey and in Hong Kong.
Sadly, he has not had the best luck but I take this opportunity of
expressing my hope that through the publicity which this book may
receive, he will achieve his lifetime's ambition.

LORD GRAHAM OF EDMONTON

States of Jersey

FROM:

Senator Terry Le Main
Royal Court House
Royal Square
St Helier
Jersey, JE1 1DD

5th October 1995

<u>To Whom It May Concern</u>

I have known Doug Woolley for a number of years and have offered and given him all the help possible to overcome bureaucratic, legal and other problems through the Courts in Jersey. I have no doubt in my mind that Doug has had a very bad deal and that he has been badly treated, misled or otherwise by persons, companies and the legal system and I have never known a more determined, tenacious gentleman in pursuing his rights and I can only hope that this autobiography will give Doug the just publicity to further his cause, whereby he could achieve his lifetime's ambition to get the transaction through that he was promised by contract.

Terry Le Main
Senator, States of Jersey

JUDICIAL GREFFE

BURRARD HOUSE,
DON STREET,
ST. HELIER,
JERSEY JE2 4TR.

D.J. Woolley, Esq.,

17th October, 1995

Dear Mr. Woolley,

Thank you for your letter of 12th October, 1995.

I am pleased to see the progress which you are making with your book and I hope that this enables you to raise sufficient funds for your salvage project.

Towards the end of your letter you write, "can you advise me" but I am not clear as to what you are asking advice on as thereafter you write, "the Courts cannot help me in the normal way". If you are asking for advice in relation to sending the bill for salvage to certain parties then I can only say that that would be a method of providing those parties with details of the value of your claim. In other words, where you previously merely had a claim for general damages you would now have a claim for an actual sum of damages. However, apart from that, you would still have the same difficulties as you have previously experienced in relation to your claim.

I hope that I have answered the right question and once again may I wish you every success with the book project. From the notes which you sent to me it seems to me that your story has very many interesting twists but merely lacks, to-date, a happy ending!

Yours sincerely,

B. I'm L Myun

B.I. Le Marquand
Judicial Greffier

HK.SC 500/5/13-111
HK SC 115/436/74.

6

Douglas John Faulkner-Woolley
THE NOT SO ORDINARY MAN

Douglas Woolley has been obsessed for years with the thought of refloating two of Southampton's ships, the Queen Elizabeth and the Titanic. He claims salvage rights on the vessels and has formed a company to do the work. But as Clive Amphlett discovered when he called at Mr Woolley's home, time is running out.

Douglas Woolley's terrace house at Essex is a long way from the sea. But every room has nautical memorabilia- picture of ships, models and documents of ships. Now aged 62 and the veteran of many jobs over the years, he is a contented bachelor. He is devoted to his dog Flint and explains "I never married but you could say I am married to an idea."

The idea is one which has filled every waking hour for most of his life., and then using the experience gained, to raise the Titanic.

Hong Kong returns to Chinese rule and the chances of getting at the Elizabeth will fade completely, unless Douglas Woolley can either do the job first or persuade the chinese to say 'yes'.

The idea would daunt lesser man, but Woolley says he obtained the salvage rights. He now plans by going straight in and asking permission.

He estimates the cost of raising the QE1 at around £18 million. He hopes to publish his biography shortly.

"You don't expect to get all the capital from a book" he explains. "But it should be sufficient to get other people interested in the project and offer financial support." Tackling the impossible and and turning up the unusual, is a Woolley's speciality.

On Sunday, 4th February 1994 he met up with a sister he had never seen before. Ann Copsey of Chigwell was the daughter of Eric Francis Faulkner, Doug's father. "I was born on the wrong side of the sheets you might say" says Mr Woolley, "the result of an affair Eric Faulkner and my mother."

"I long suspected there was a sister from the things people in the family said, but took me a long time to trace her."

The re-union went well. They intend to meet me again." We thought we could

DOUGLAS JOHN FAULKNER-WOOLLEY

Douglas family

7

see a family likeness between us. It was a weird experience but we got along well."

For Douglas Woolley it was just another example of how tenacity and attention to detail can produce results.

Even the way in which he first became interested in the Titanic was marked by the bizarre incident.

He had two great aunts, Sally and Ellen, who had booked a passage on the Titanic. Their many belongings were on board, when as the result of a premonition the night before, they decided the vessel was doomed. They did not sail, but it was too late for their possessions, which went to the bottom when the Titanic struck an iceberg and foundered on 14th April 1912. Douglas Woolley did not know the aunts very well. But as a small boy, the incident got him hooked on the Titanic and thoughts of salvaging her.

Today his company, the Titanic and Seawise Salvage Company, is poised to carry out the work, with the boy he fostered, Steven Bilsby, in-charge of diving operation. But just getting the ships up to the surface is difficult enough. On top of this, Douglas Woolley has also fought a lengthy battle in the courts for compensation against Salvors of Jersey, with whom he says he signed a contract they did not carry out. When he heard that the QE1, then re-named the Seawise University, had sunk in Hong Kong harbour after a fire on board, he approached its owner Mr C. Y. Tung and asked for permission to salvage her. Tung, he says, gave him the go-ahead. As a result, he was subsequently approached by a group of businessmen with whom the deal for lifting her was signed. Salvors, he discovered did not exist at the time of the signing, but was set-up shortly afterwards. At the time this task would have cost £14,000.

Today somewhere around £19 million would be a more realistic figure.

Woolley later went to Hong Kong to find out what, if anything, was happening.

He claims he was threatened and harassed by the Salvor company and that efforts were made to prevent him returning to the UK. He sees the re-floating of the QE1 as a venture which would to some extent be self-financing. On- board the vessel when it went down were 40,000 tons of oil, which could be sold off on recovery to help pay for the work.

As he roams his house, talking about the project, Douglas Woolley produces files and letters. They are from courts in both Hong Kong and Jersey,from B.I.Le Marquand, Judicial Greffier of the Royal Court of Jersey and many others wishing him success.

Lord Graham of Edmonton, opposition Chief Whip to the House of Lords, in 1995 says in a foreword to the book, he has been happy to intercede with authorities in both Jersey and Hong Kong on Doug's behalf. "I take this opportunity of expressing my hope that through the publicity which this book may receive, he (Douglas Woolley) achieves his lifetime's ambition."

Appropriately the biography of Douglas Woolley is entitled "Douglas J. Faulkner Woolley, One Man's Dream" and has been written by two members of his family, Clive and R.J. Amphlett.

At the moment four copies exist, but confidential talks are under way which, says Mr Woolley, should produce the finance for publication.

After that, it is full steam-ahead for Hong Kong harbour and the prize that lies at the bottom.

hopes of refloating Queen Elizabeth

A MAN who claims he owns the salvage rights to the Queen Elizabeth is trying to get the Royal Court to order three Jersey businessmen to re-float her and sail her back to Jersey or Southampton

However, his efforts have suffered a temporary set back as Deputy Bailiff Mr Vernon Tomes has refused to sign his Order ...

Douglas Woolley, a waiter in ...

He claims that the three men have failed to meet the contract and he wants the Royal Court to order them to fulfil it and to bring the ship home to Jersey or Southampton

But Mr Tomes has refused to sign Mr Woolley's Order of Justice and, therefore, he cannot bring the case to Court

Mr Woolley has now requested the Royal Court to direct that the Order of Justice be signed ...

Douglas John Faulkner-Woolley
THE NOT SO ORDINARY MAN

Born July 1936 in Gambia Terrace, Liverpool (now part of the Anglican Cathedral property), Douglas John Woolley, was the eldest of three children. His mother was born in 1916, in a little village called Cardington, Shropshire (Salop). She went to the local school and later the family moved to a nearby village called Bromfield where they lived in a cottage called 'The Decoy.' This is where Gwen's mother became very ill and died. This was a sad loss to Gwen who was only 17 at the time and was left to be brought up by her father. Doug's father was Eric Francis Faulkner.

When Gwen was 19 years old, she left home to go and live in Hereford, but because of the lack of work there she decided to move again, this time to Liverpool. She found a job in Bootle, in a laundry, until war broke-out and she went to work in a weapons factory.

Because of the war, it was no longer safe for children to stay in big cities like London and Liverpool.. In 1939, he was sent to live with his grandfather in Worthen, Shropshire.

Back in the countryside it was still quite safe and the children could play without too much fear, although Douglas remembers that they did find one bomb in a farmer's field behind where they lived.

He later went to school in Worthen aged 6, and his head master was Tomy Hennry. This was where Doug first found the desire to raise the R.M.S. Titanic.

Life in Worthen was good. The vicar was the Reverend Canon Bell and he told Doug about the bible and to have faith in God.

'And when it was day they knew not the land; but they discovered a certain creek with a shore into which they were minded, if it were possible to steer the ship.'

His grandfather's name was George Woolley, but most of the people in the village called him Pops.

Pops served in the 1914 war with the King's Shropshire Light Infantry (K.S.L.I.) and Doug also served with the (K.S.L.I.) for a short term. He had lots of stories to tell about the war. Eric was also in the K.S.L.I at Shrewsbury.

(A present-day photo of Douglas with his mother)
Douglas John Faulkner-Woolley; Eric Francis Faulkner-Gwendoline Louise Woolley; Francis Herbert Faulkner-Ida May Amphlett; John Amphlett -Eliza Merideth; William Amphlett-Susanna Clemson.

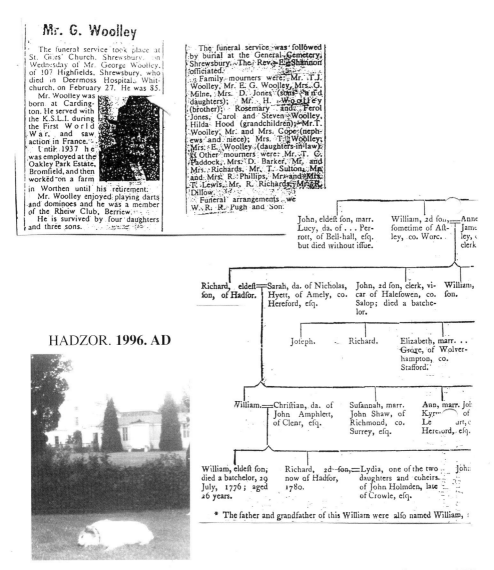

Mr. G. Woolley

The funeral service took place at St. Giles' Church, Shrewsbury, on Wednesday of Mr. George Woolley, of 107 Highfields, Shrewsbury, who died in Deermoss Hospital, Whitchurch, on February 27. He was 85.

Mr. Woolley was born at Cardington. He served with the K.S.L.I. during the First World War, and saw action in France.

Until 1937 he was employed at the Oakley Park Estate, Bromfield, and then worked on a farm in Worthen until his retirement.

Mr. Woolley enjoyed playing darts and dominoes and he was a member of the Rheiw Club, Berriew.

He is survived by four daughters and three sons.

The funeral service was followed by burial at the General Cemetery, Shrewsbury. The Rev. E. Shannon officiated.

Family mourners were: Mr. T.J. Woolley, Mr. E. G. Woolley, Mrs. G. Milne, Mrs. D. Jones (sons and daughters); Mr. H. Woolley (brother); Rosemary and Ferol Jones, Carol and Steven Woolley, Hilda Hood (grandchildren); Mr. T. Woolley, Mr. and Mrs. Cope (nephews and niece); Mrs. T. Woolley, Mrs. E. Woolley (daughters-in-law). Other mourners were: Mr. T. C. Paddock, Mrs. D. Barker, Mr. and Mrs. Richards, Mr. T. Sutton, Mr. and Mrs. R. Phillips, Mr. and Mrs. T. Lewis, Mr. R. Richards, Mr. R. Dillow.

Funeral arrangements were W. R. R. Pugh and Son.

HADZOR. 1996. AD

Edward Faulkner (aged 32) from Ebbw Vale, buried in 1907; Martha Faulkner (aged 79) from Leintwardline, buried in 1926; Jjohn GeorgeFaulkner (aged 77) also from Leintwardline, buried in 1927; and the ashes of W. Faulkner (aged 85) from London, buried in the grave of John and Martha Faulkner.

The Parish of Wigmore Abbey.

Downton Church

11

THE FAMILY TREE

FINCH - CHAMBERS - WOOLLEY
CADWALLADR

FROM HANLEY - SALOP AND CARDINGTON - SALOP 1765 TO 1995

KING UTHER

CHAMBERS - ACVIDER EDWIN

PENDRAGON

See book King Arthur the true story, death 519 AD

CADWALLADR
EDWARD & ELIZABETH

ARTHUR CHAMBERS (M)
(of River Mead) MARIA SHORT

CADWALLADR (M) MARIA FINCH - MARTHA FINCH
(WIFE OF THOMAS WOOLLEY) (Grandparents)

FINCH

AMPHLETTS

KEVIN PRICE

LOUISE MARY CHAMBERS (M)

GEORGE WOOLLEY

Grandparents

NANCY & MARIA
(Sisters)

GWENDOLYN L WOOLLEY

DOUGLAS JOHN WOOLLEY

AMPHLETTS

FATHER LAID TO REST AT
BROMFIELD PARISH CHURCH

GWENDOLYN L WOOLLEY
born 1916

DOUGLAS JOHN WOOLLEY
born 20 July 1936 AD, LIVERPOOL SOUTH

FUNERAL REGISTER. BEIBL SANCTAIDD

Thomas Woolley 1904. Martha Carter (Finch) 1940. George Woolley 1970.
George Hood 1961. W-Rodger Woolf 1995
FAMILY NAMES:
WOOLLEY:CADWALLADR:FINCH:CHAMBERS:RICARDE:HOOD:PRICE:SHORT

12

```
ROYAL COURT OF JERSEY CI (17.1.D.J.F-W)
            ORDER OF JUSTICE


This order of justice,declaration of judgement

DOUGLAS JOHN FAULKNER-WOOLLEY,PLAINTIFF
                    V
OFFSHORE MANAGEMENT LTD    1/DEFENDANTS
SALVORS INTERNATIONAL LTD 2/      "
MR BRIAN HAMILTON          3/     "
MR(CAPT) STEPHEN KINGLEY  4/      "
This order of justice and declaration judgment
is to ask the court to confirm the fact that
there was a contract (and is) made in Jersey CI
28/29-4/1972 I ask the Royal Court to give notice
that there was and is a salvage contract on the
QE1 (seawise university) in (GB)HONG KONG.
The contract is still in exisrence and is
enforcable,(for refs see, know your rights-Readers
Digest 1997)(and bill of senator Lowel Weicker
US 21 oct 1986) to be affected by the viscount
or one of his duly sworne officers.
```

William Amphlett Salwarpe Ombersley 1580.
William Amphlett Hadzor 1620.
William Amphlett Salwarpe 1520.
William Amphlett Sparry 1662 Hadzor.
Richard - Anne Cookes 1624.
John Amphlett Lucy Perott of Hadzor and Clent 1656.
John Amphlett Alice Powell.
William Amphlett Elizabeth Treece 1730.
William Amphlett Susanna Glemson of Wrckwardline.
John Apmhlett Elizabeth Merideth.
Ida May Amphlett Francis Herbert Faulkner.
Eric Francis Faulkner 1913 Gwendoline L Woolley 1916.
Douglas John Faulkner-Woolley 1936.
Eric Francis Faulkner 1913 Dorris May Thomas 1986.
Anne Hazel Copsey Michael Copsey
John Francis Faulkner Copsey
Thomas Woolley 1904 Martha Carter 1940 Alfred Chamber
George Woolley Louise Mary Chambers 1934 - 1970
Eric Francis Faulkner Gwendolien Louise.
Douglas John Faulkner-Woolley b 1936.

13

NAME OF SHIP *Titanic*

Whether a Sailing or Steam Ship; if Steam how propelled.	Where built	When built	Name and Address of Builder
Steamship Triple screw	Belfast	1912.	Harland and Wolff Ld. Belfast.

			FEET.	TENTHS.
Number of Decks	...	...		
Number of Masts	...	...		
Rigged	...	...		
Stem	...	...		
Build	...	...		
Galleries	...	...		
Head	...	...		
Framework and description of Vessel	steel		
Number of Bulkheads	fifteen		
Number of water ballast tanks and their capacity in tons			

Length from forepart of stem under the bowsprit to the aft side of the head of the stern post ... 852 5
Length at quarter of depth from top of weather deck at side amidships to bottom of keel ... 849 2
Main breadth to outside of plank 92 5
Depth in hold from tonnage deck to ceiling at midships ... 31 6
Depth in hold from upper deck to ceiling at midships, in the case of three decks and upwards ... 59 5.8
Depth from top of beam amidships to top of keel ... 64 9.1
Depth from top of deck at sides amidships to bottom of keel ... 65 5.3
Round of beam 2.5
Length of engine room: (if any) 123

PARTICULARS OF DISPLACEMENT.

Total to quarter the depth from weather deck at side amidships to bottom of keel ... 180 tons

PARTICULARS OF PROPELLING ENGINES, &c. (if any).

Whether British or Foreign made.	When made.	Name and Address of Makers.
Engines. British	Engines. 1912	Harland & Wolff Ld.
Boilers. British	Boilers. 1912	Boilers. Belfast.

Ditto per inch immersion at same depth.

	Reciprocating Engines.		Rotary Engines.		N. H. P. I. H. P. Speed of Ship.
	No. and diameter of cylinder in each set.	Length of Stroke.	No. of Cylinders in each set.		
	1–54 1–96 2–97	45'	0 × 0		6906 50,000 21 knots

Note.—1. The tonnage of the engine room spaces below the approximate...

(Signed) W. H. Chapman   G. Registrar.

Col. 14

SUMMARY.

Col. 9.	Col. 10.	Col. 11.	Col. 12	Col. 13.
Number of Transactions.	Name of Owners.	Mortgages and Certificate of Mortgage.	Names of Mortgagees and Attorneys under Certificate of Mortgage.	Date of Transactions. Numbers of Transactions.
				Numbers of Shares held.

Pops' father was Thomas Woolley and his mother Martha Carter and they came from Hanley, Shropshire. He also had an uncle who was a solicitor to Queen Victoria - Pops was very proud of the fact that his uncle served the Queen. This is where Doug probably gets his legal mind from. After the war Pops went back to his proper trade of farming; He was also a grave-digger for the local church, swept chimneys and was a champion thatcher. When Doug went to live with Pops, Pops' sons Arthur, Thom and Ted were still living at home.

He told me that life with his grandad was hard, but an reflection was the best time of his life, as grandad used to tell him so many stories about himself and the family The Amphletts. (A-B)

One story was about his two great aunts, whose names were Sally and Ellen (better known as Nel.) They had booked a passage on the *Titanic,* but because of a premonition they decided not to board the ship as they were sure it was doomed. But it was too late for their belongings, as they had already been placed on board and were soon to be lost for ever, for on 10th April 1972 the Titanic left on her maiden voyage from Southampton to New York, stopping at Cherbourg, France and Queenstown, South Ireland. On 14th April 1912 the "Unsinkable" Titanic hit an iceberg while travelling at 21kph. The time was about 11.40pm. The iceberg made a 300ft gash through five of her watertight compartments and only took about 2 1/2 hours to sink, leaving only a third of the 2,227 people on board to survive. This meant that in all 1,513 people lost their lives, which included five Chinese stowaways,

and Rex the dog lost his life helping others, on 15th April 1912. When Doug was told the story, he didn't know too much about his great aunts, but it was enough to get him hooked on the Titanic. As he grew up, so did his passion for the ship and by the time he was 12 years old he had acquired extensive knowledge of the R.M.S. Titanic and found a possible way in which to raise her from the watery grave where she spent so long.

(Douglas' grandfather - a darts and domino player at the Rheiw Club, Berriew)

(Douglas with Mr A. Wakefield and Flint)

He felt then and, to this day, still feels that to raise the Titanic, tow her to New York so as to finish her journey and then bring her back to Southampton, England, would be a more fitting way to remember the tragic loss of so many people, rather than to leave her buried at the bottom of the ocean 2.5 miles down.

Grandad also read him stories from a book which included 'Rumpelstiltskin', 'The Cock of the North', 'Mr Nobody' and Captain Smith', but still insists to this day that the best one was the story about 'Captain Smith'.

(Douglas at 12 years old, with his brother George)

(Douglas' grandfather with Auntie Mary, George & Hilda - Douglas' brother and Sister)

(Wood House Shropshire) at Bomfield Salop. Home of Woolley's family in 1930 AD.

(Judge Amphlett - J. P. QC)

16

THE RAISING OF THE TITANIC

THE TITANIC DISASTER

The sinking of the White Star Liner's Titanic on 15th April 1912 while on her maiden voyage was one of the most terrible sea disasters of all time, with 1,502 people losing their lives.

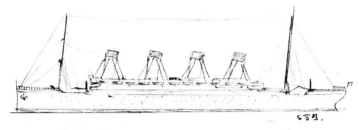

(THE SIDE OF THE TITANIC)
and
(AND THE TOP OF THE TITANIC)

A Practice before the real thing?

Another famous and ill-fated liner made the headlines recently, the ex-Cunarder Queen Elizabeth. Mr Woolley sees the burnt-out wreck lying in comparatively shallow water in Hong Kong harbour as the kind of opportunity he has been waiting for to prove his methods really work.

He wrote immediately to the owner, Mr. C. Y. Tung, who plans for the project.

He sees this as a 'dress rehearsal' before the final performance, the major job, the raising of the Titanic. The project, expected to cost over £1.5 million, would be tackled using the same method - hydrogen - filled containers - although the Queen Elizabeth is lying in shallow water, with parts of her still showing above the surface.

Should he be granted permission to go ahead with this 'dress run' it would throw open, to the full public gaze, the technical knowhow of this team.

Nevertheless the Titanic would still remain the dream of a lifetime, and Mr. Woolley sees no reason why he should not have his liner safely beached at Cape Race by next autumn.

He hopes that in time he can bring her back to Liverpool. There she can be set up in dry dock and refitted as a maritime museum, school and conference centre.

There is absolutely no room for doubt in Mr. Woolley's mind that he will over come the difficulties believed insuperable by Titanic's first owners, the White Star Line, and that one day soon his ship will rise from watery grave.

When the war had ended Doug went to live with his mother in Liverpool. He attended Lister Drive School in Old Swan, Liverpool and that is where he started doing some test work to find the best method to raise the Titanic. He eventually came up with the idea that if he could make some pontoons and be able to anchor them to the bottom of the ship he might just be able to raise it. He did his calculations and found that he would need 200 pontoons evenly placed around the ship because the Titanic was a dead weight of 66,000 tones. The pontoons would be anchored together by nylon rope, but each length of rope would have to have a breaking strain of 200 tones. Once all the pontoons were in place, then the surface ships would start to generate the 20 megawatt of electricity to power the charge that is needed to inflate the pontoons with 85,555 cubic yards of hydrogen, which would then send the electricity down to the leading pontoon. This charge done by a negative and positive cable running down 2.5 miles to the leading pontoon sending a 20 megawatt charge down to inflate the pontoons, but at the same time sending an ultrasonic sound-wave to the sea bed in order to shake the ship from the sediment of the muddy sea bed. It would then take between 7-14 days to raise so as not to cause any damage to what is left of the ship.How did the birth of the Titanic and her two sister ships originate?

Back in 1907 there was a meeting between Bruce Ismay, Chairman of the White Star Line and Ismay Imrie and Co, and Lord Pirrie of Harland Wolff, the Morgan shipping empire of America. This meeting took place at a house in Belgrave Square followed by other meetings in the White Star offices in Liverpool at the pier head. The result of these late night meetings were the planned building of the three sister ships Olympic, Titanic and Britannic- the largest ships ever to be built at that time. These were the ships which caused and demise of White Star Line to be merged with Cunard which become Cunard White Star.

The Olympic first set sail an 31 May 1911 from Southampton to New York and was a new breed of ship for the athletically minded, for on board she catered for sports, such as the first swimming pool on a ship, plus electric horses, bicycles, rowing machines and next to the swimming pool they had a Turkish bath with a sauna as well as full time masseuse, also a vibrating belt for helping to remove extra flab! The Titanic had the same - and more.

In 1914, the Titanic's second sister ship, the Britannic was launched and was immediately commissioned for use in the First World War as a Red Cross vessel but she had a short life, as she was hit by a German ship, believed to be in the Aegean sea. Britannic was later examined by famous deep-sea diver Jacques-Yves Cousteau.

By this time Doug had set about the task of obtaining the rights of the ship and its contents. Some of the contents believed to be aboard the Titanic were estimated wealth of the 10 millionaires on board - £120,000,000, De Beer diamond - £175,000,000, Jewelled book of the Rubayiat of Omar Khayhamm - £250,000, plus the black Buddah of Tibet which is priceless (this was said to have been stolen from the Dalai Lama). There are many other items, including 30 veteran cars and encrusted Papal Cross, also seven parcels of parchment of the Hebrew Holly Bible and a set of bagpipes.

Doug reported the fact to the media and was given the recognition for the facts in 1960/70 which made him known in the shipping world, and also became a household name. The press coverage he received was world- wide and because of it he was asked to do a lecture at Liverpool University on the salvage of the Titanic which was very well received. He also had invitations from several television stations to appear on their shows. One such programme that springs to Doug's mind was when he did a News programme in July 1974 for CITV in Jersey.

Doug's claim is based on complexities of mercantile law no expert cares to challenge. He approached the Board of Trade, who told him Cunard were the owners, but he would need to search diligently until he found out who all the owners of the property were if he was to succeed. This he did.

Contact with Cunard White Star resulted in the reaction that it was nothing to do with them. The Titanic was only insured to a quarter of its value (Mainly because it was thought to be unsinkable). Eventually Doug traced the underwriters in Sheffield who had the rights and gave them to Doug . It was possible that they did this because they did not think it possible to raise the Titanic (he said). He also

obtained similar waivers from the descendants of those who had property on board. This activity resulted in a lot of press coverage which in turn brought him a pile of correspondence from people offering help.

One letter came from Hungary where a group of scientists had been working in Budapest on a similar plan for another ship, and thought they might be of help. They studied Doug's proposals and carried out tests on the Danube over a three year period before reporting back that it was feasible.

In 1951 Doug got a job at the Stroudgre Telephone company in Edge Lane. He worked there for about six months then found a job in a sheet metal factory in Knowsley, but this only lasted for nine weeks. He then worked for Dunlop for a couple of weeks before moving back. He started working for a local farmer, Mr. David Rowlands, who was also a friend of the family. He worked for him for about seven years and his starting pay was £2 a week.

Doug told me that he remembered going down to the signal box at Briedden, near Welshpool, to talk to the signalman who worked there. He said that one day the signalman had a letter for him and told him to take it to the station master at Welshpool which he did without question. What Doug did not know was that the letter was about him and was a letter of introduction. The station master read it, then turned round to Doug and offered him a job in the signal box, which he accepted. He was then given another letter to take back to the signalman and was told what to do. Doug stayed there for about seven years.

During this period Doug was having problems with his family, as they poo-pooed all that he was trying to do. The only one who gave him any encouragement was Pop's. He goes on to say that at times, he felt very much out in the cold and also very much alone. Because of this he decided to move to the big city and try his luck there. Times were very hard and he had to sell off all his belongings to make ends meet until he started his new job, which took him about two weeks to find. It was Moss Bros, the outfitters, who gave him that start and he was then able to get a bedsit on the Caledonian Road.

His next job was helping a painter and decorator, but he did not feel at home in London and moved to Baldock. He housed in Park Street and found employment with Kayser Bondor. He worked there until 'the contract' that was made in 1972.

During that time he tended the local church clock, making sure that it was always wound up.

Whilst living in Baldock, Doug remembers that he met some friends out side the local Chip shop and suggested that they go up to Liverpool that night for a friends 21st Birthday party, Which they did. The four friends set off for Liverpool in an instant and drove straight to the place where the party was being held. No one else knew they had gone, but within 30 minutes of Doug arriving at the party he received a phone call from some Jersey businessmen. Doug did not think at the time to ask them how they knew he was at the party that night, as it had only been a last minute decision and they had told no one else where they were going. Doug now feels that they must have been keeping a close watch on him and had him followed, from Baldock - Herts to Old Swan, Liverpool.

They told him to go Southampton and get on the plane that was waiting for him at the airport to take him to Jersey, as it was of the utmost importance that they signed a contract as soon as possible. Doug did not ask any questions at this time, did as they asked and went to Southampton were he was met by Captain Stephen Kingsley. They boarded the waiting plane and were met at Jersey airport by Mr. Brian Hamilton and others. (He found out later that the others were directors of Salvors and another firm who were party to the contract.) They then took Doug to an address in La Motte Street, St Helier, Jersey, C.I. As well as Doug's, the other names on the contract were Mr. Kingsley, Mr. Hamilton and others.

The trip was all paid for by the Jersey businessmen and they told Doug not to worry about a thing as it was all taken care of. He was very bemused by the whole thing and did not know quite what to think. He never bothered to try and find out why the Seawise University (QE1) had been set on fire. All he could think about was that this was going to be the start of his dream coming true, only to find that it was not in the plan to actually salvage the Seawise for whatever reasons they had. He later found out that these so-called Jersey businessmen had carried out work for Mr. Tung before they had ever contacted

Doug, but his findings did not come until years later. One thing was for sure - they did not intend to tell Doug their true plans.

(Steven and the offices of Salvors & Offshore Management Ltd in Jersey, C.I.)

What I think, as the author, and what is on the tip of everyone's tongue, is why was the Seawise set on fire in the first place? What secrets have been buried in Hong Kong harbour and who are they trying to protect? Why won't they let it be salvaged? Is it the government itself who is hiding a big secret?

My theory is that when the QE1 was sold to America to be turned into a floating hotel, they realised that it would not make much money, so to save face they then sold it on to a Mr C.Y. Tung who had the job of getting the QE1 from America to Hong Kong. It had to be towed as it was only running on one engine and they had to stop in Africa to make general repairs before it could continue it's voyage. I believe that it was here that something was put aboard that was of the utmost secrecy, but the secret was leaked from as long ago as 1960 the Titanic salvage project was set up by Doug with the help of

Philip Slade and later helped along further by Clive Ramsay and Joe Wilkins, also a company by the name of Aquatech Safety and Diving ENGINEERS Ltd. The Directors were Mr Green and Mr Fred Clark. These people, and a host of others, are now to be named. Those, who in the beginning thought that they would be all it would take to get the ball rolling are as follows:

Lord Bristol, Philip Slade, Szaszko Lazslo, Dr Balas Ambrus, Peter Goodwin, Jim O'Donnell, Antony Cathart, Tony Hatt, Clive Ramsay, Adam Tang, Hugh Carlon, Stephen Neodes, Peter Webster, John dade Dennis Bisset, Bill Bisset & Dave Williams.

In 1977, a group of West Berlin businessmen set up Titanic-Tresor as backing to the project that Doug started in the 1960s. A meeting was held in Berlin but Doug told Mr Slade he was not content with the offer made; contact was withdrawn and no further offers were made.

It was at this time that Mr Tantum and Dr Ballard set up the company called Seaonics Inc. Mr Slade and Mr Ramsay were also very busy at this time contacting a Mr Derek Berwin and Commander John Gratton of Fathom Line Ltd. Also at that time Mr Slade made contact with sir James Goldsmith, owner of Now magazine, with a proposal of selling the story rights of the Titanic survey. It was agreed that £25,000 would be an initial payment; this sum was believed to have been paid but never accounted for. Goldsmith was never told about Doug's involvement or of the meetings held with the Daily Mirror group and also of meetings held in Berlin

21

and New York. Goldsmith was also not aware of the QE1 and Titanic contract made in Jersey in 1972. But some twenty years later these names are no longer part of today's team as the going got tough, and so much money was made but not accounted for. Doug said that he believes that Sir James Goldsmith's part in all this is that of an innocent bystander.

One of the newest members of Doug's team is a friend, Graham Mead. He was born in the county of Essex on 20th July 1969. His education started at Haselmere Infant and then Haselmere Junior school; he then attended the Sir Charles Lucas senior school and when he left he achieved four CSEs which was enough for him to enter a one year engineering course. At the end of the course he was graded and passed E.I.T.B. which was enough for a placement at a firm called 'Sound Attenuators' and they offered him a four year apprenticeship which he completed and gained his City And Guilds in many different levels of engineering. At this time he was offered a full-time job as a maintenance fitter, but after three years was made redundant. It was not easy looking for work at a time when jobs were few and far between. Graham decided to move from Essex and try his luck in Chatteris, but it was still about a year before he found work, by which time he had moved a village called Manea and this is where he was introduced to Doug.

He met Doug again at his wife's party and had a chat with him but was not too interested in what Doug was doing at that time. About a year later Doug had decided to move to Chattris and it was Graham who offered to move him. It was from this moment that he first showed sign of interest in Doug and his plans, and soon realised that he would like to be part of the team and it was agreed that he would look after the filming side of things and also help Steven on the diving side.

Another, not so new, member of the team is Doug's beloved pet dog, Flint, who has been with Doug since he was three weeks old. He is now 14 years old and has been spoiled all his life. Doug says he is only number one after Steven, but he loves the dog like a son. He attained third in the Chatteris Dog Show in June 1995, which was the first dog show he had ever entered. Flint's birthday falls on the same day as the company 'Salvors' was formed in Jersey on 4th May, also the date Doug's great grandmother died at Cardington Salop with her son, grandad's brother W.H. Woolley at her bedside. She at one time lived at Rushbury Wall, Salop.

The following is extracted from papers of one of the hearings in the Royal Court, Jersey, C.I.

Mr. Woolley:
I'm asking the Court a question, and all I require is an answer to a question. The question is this. If a contract is made between two individuals four days before the limited company is formed, although we were led to believe that it was already formed, who is the contract with?

President:
I think the answer that we would......I don't think we're really here to conduct a tutorial.

Mr. Woolley:
No, but I am surely entitled to an answer.

President:
I think the answer that you would be entitled to have if you put that question is that one person who, on those facts is not likely to be liable is the company.

Mr Woolley:
Thank you.

President:
The only people who might or might not be liable would be the individuals with whom you were dealing.

Mr. Woolley:
That's right

President:
But that may well have been a good reason for your suing the individuals, but that isn't what you did.

Mr. Woolley:
I know I didn't do that but it was because of the circumstances at the time that I wasn't given the facts. Now, I've asked the question, you've actually give me the answer that I required. It's no good smiling!

President:
Well, I was just thinking that at least it was of some advantage you coming here today if you got the advice for nothing!

The following is from another hearing:

Mr. Woolley:
Can I just ask you something else while we, you know, the sort of thing which happens.

President:
Yes.

Mr. Woolley:
I have had several letters from Mr Habin. I would like to know in all of these who does Mr. Habin represent. May I ask the question?

President:
Are you asking Mr. Habin through us?

Mr. Woolley:
I am asking........Well, can I ask Mr Habin direct?

President:
Mr. Habin can you assist......

Advocate Habin ... (indistinct)

President:
I know you are representing the respondent but do you want to be more particular?

Mr. Woolley:
Yes.

President:
No, no I am asking Mr Habin now, you have asked me to ask him and I am asking him.

Adv Habin:
I am representing the respondent in this particular action, Sir.

President:
Yes.

Adv Habin:
Mr Forrest and no one else.....

President:
Mr. Forrest.

Mr. Woolley:
Well, why then you have involved Salvors International Limited in your letters to me?

President:
Mr. Habin, can you help about that?

Adv Habin:
I have referred to the company......
(Mr Habin, Advocate of the Royal Court stated (Salvors) is a company which is involved in the particular action. By this act advocate Habin accepted the contract of 1972 on the Titanic and the QE1 in Hong Kong on behalf of Kingsley-Hamilton and others.)

Mr Woolley:
.....How we were put into a hotel in London and kept for almost two years by Mr. Hamiliton and Mr. Kingsley. How we used to get, I used to get, a series of threatening phone calls from these people. I was threatened with an injunction from Mr. Michael Forrest who was a partner of theirs in all this. Now, I've never mentioned Mr. Forrest, only in a minor way once before when I asked the Court could I in fact sue Mr. Michael Forrest for part in all this. I asked the question "can I ask the Court a question, the founders of the company Salvors International Limited were a Mr Michael Forrest, a Mr Stephen Kingsley and Mr Brian Hamliton. They formed a company and I have brought an action, was it possible in bringing the action. Could I in fact sue the three parties concerned because they were founders". Now the Deputy Bailiff says yes that could have been done in 1974. Now Mr Hamilton tells me that he had nothing to do with any company. In fact he said to me in a letter which you have in the file, hence the reason why they've been put in here, that he had nothing to do with.... "I have very distant recollection that this was to be involved the (indistinct) attempt to raise the Titanic". That is Mr Forrest's words. "I also recollect that my firm was not involved" - I never even said it was. But when Mr Forrest writes to me, he always writes to me on his company, his own company, letter headed paper. That is the only involvement as far as he was concerned excepting on a Royal Court document Mr Michael Forrest's name appears as a co-founder of Salvors International Limited.

A contract for the survey and salvage of
the wreck QE1 was agreed and taken over
on behalf of Mr Douglas John Woolley
and his project by Captain Kingsley and
Mr Brian Hamilton of Salvors Limited of
Jersey, Channel Islands on 29th April.
Also included in this contract, work was to
commence with immediate effect on the
Titanic stage of the project.

At the Avon Court Hotel, London, this
above agreement and fact was confirmed
at a meeting. In attendance at the same
meeting were Mr Philip Slade, Captain
Kingsley, Mr Hamilton, Mr Peter Bajic
and Mr Douglas John Woolley.
Photographs of the QE1 were shown to all
in attendance at same. The outcome of the
meeting was that nothing was under taken
by Salvors Limited to complete their side
of the contract. This was a serious case of
a breach of contract on their behalf. Mr
Peter Bajic put Mr Douglas John Woolley
in the Ginestar House Hotel, Cromwell
Road, all expenses paid for by the same.

Shortly after the above taking place, Mr
Douglas John Woolley was offered an
appointment as a manger of a Hotel
belonging to Salvors Limited in conjunc-
tion with the Titanic project. Mr Woolley
began to receive threatening telephone
calls, from a person or persons unknown,
towards the latter end of October 1972.
The Jersey Company was always mentioned in these calls. Mr Douglas John
Woolley was repeatedly warned to "lay-
off" the QE1 wreck in Hong Kong, China.

Hong Kong News 1972
Report on Salvage Plans
of the QE1
and Mr Douglas John Faulkner Woolley

25

The following is an extract from a newspaper report from Dougs's Press Diary:

'It costs London ratepayers a staggering £250,000 a month to keep 1,250 families who have no homes of their own in bed and breakfast accommodation. And two men with three Bed and Breakfast properties say they have an income of £100,000 a year from them.

Mr Peter Bajic (and another) administer these hotels for the homeless.

"We have a reasonable and responsible attitude but we're in it for the money".

Two of the properties are on short leases and the other is run on a management basis.

The Council asked us if we could take a homeless family. They were booked in on a nightly basis-but they were still there six months later.

It was said that income from fifty homeless families for the three properties was around £2000 a week. The weekly expenditure is about £1,200 and out of that Peter and I draw £800 wages each. With those figures it might appear as though we are stashing away an extra £600 or £700 a week, but that's not true.

"At the moment we are still in debt, but in six months to a year we hope our gross capital expenditure will have come to an end. From then on we will start making money. Over about two and half years we should make about £62,000 profit."

(Peter Bajic was a member of Salvors Limited of Jersey, C.I.)

On 31st August 1983 information was received from a reliable source, that Mr Slade had a meeting with Mr Jack Grimm, Solicitor, in New York. Mr P. Slade denied this, but confirmed at the meeting in the presence of Mr Charles H. Betts that a meeting had been made.

£20,000 was paid to Mr Philip Slade as a Director of Seawise and Titanic Salvage and this money in turn was paid to a Director of a Company in Hayling Island. Also there is information that a national newspaper has put up £20,000 to a private individual to start a new company and go in search of the wreck Titanic in the Atlantic Ocean.

Some members have used Doug for private gain. One even tried to get him to pay a tax bill of £3,000 by putting the bill in Doug's name, which he eventually sorted out. One member of the team also borrowed £300 to pay a phone bill and get food for his dog. This money is still outstanding-like the contract in Jersey.

Now the Titanic is his.

Mr Douglas Woolley, leader of the Titanic salvage team is now the owner of the sunken liner.

Mr Gordon Laycock, Director of a Doncaster firm of the same name, has he passed over his grandfather's under-writing of the ship to Mr Woolley of Baldock.

"This is really good news," said a delighted Mr Woolley this week.

In return, Laycock Company will be named in Press and Tv reports for giving the under-writing.

"I'm sure this will be great benefit to the company, as they will receive international publicity," added Mr Woolley.

Salvage work is expected to beging next year it is planned to bring the Titanic, which sunk in 1912, back to dry-dock as a floating museum.

(The *Titanic* narrowly escapes collision as she leaves Southampton on 10 April.

The suction of her propellers tore the American liner *New York* from her moorings, an accident seemed certain until Captain Smith cut his engines.)

(Poop deck of the *Titanic*.)

Clive Ramsay

Philip Slade, one of the salvage team.

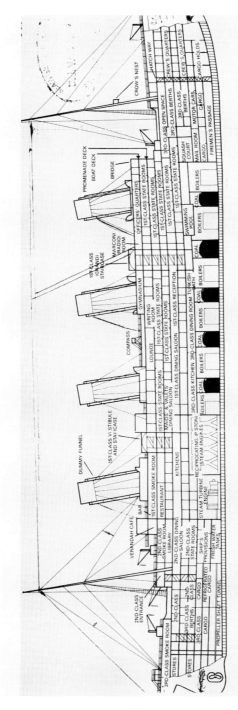

Side Plan of The R.M.S White Star Titanic 66,000 tons DW. British registered Board of Trade . Salvage plans Made in Shrewsbury and tested in Budapest. Pilot salvage on QE1 Hong Kong confirmed in Jersey C.I By Salvors and offshore management Ltd.

29

First Class
dining room
Titanic

(Flint)

(Doug and Flint)

30

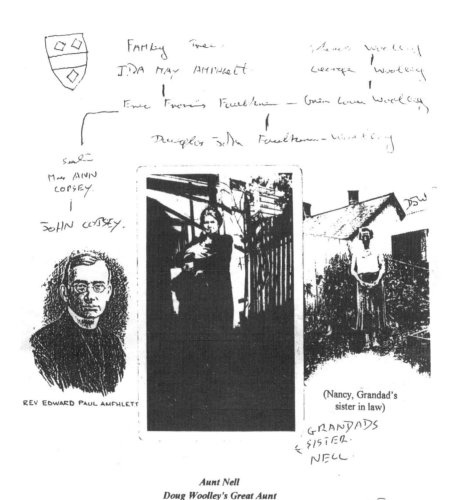

FAMILy Tree
IDA MAY AMFHLETT

Eric Francis Faulkner — Gwen Louie Woolley

Daughter Julia Faulkner — Woolley

Sarah
Mary ANN COPSEY.

JOHN COPSEY.

REV EDWARD PAUL AMFHLETT

(Nancy, Grandad's sister in law)

GRANDADS SISTER. NELL.

Aunt Nell
Doug Woolley's Great Aunt

RMS Titanic

Along with her sister, Aunt Nell was scheduled to depart on the QE1 on her maiden voyage on 10 April, 1912. Staying overnight in Southampton on 9 April, 1912, all luggage boarded, they both had a premonition that something terrible was going to happen and decided not to proceed with the journey. All their luggage went down with the White Star Titanic of 1912.

RMS TITANIC, INC.

17 BATTERY PLACE, SUITE 203, NEW YORK, NEW YORK 10004
TEL.: 212-558-6300 • FAX: 212-482-1912

Via Mail

December 7, 1995

Mr. Douglas Woolley

MR D J FAULKNER-WOOLLEY
670A GREEN LANE
GOODMAYES
ILFORD
ESSEX

Dear Douglas,

It was nice to chat with you today.

As promised, we will be delighted as the right thing to do present your story before the people of the world as we mo forward with the exhibition.

In that effort in the six months ahead we should arrange meeting between yourself and the proposed exhibition designers London.

I finally must say the "Mail" article was proof of the wor side of journalism. Indeed, "a lie can travel half way around t world before the truth has tied its shoes", as Mark Twain on said. And, as Lincoln said "the truth is the best defense". just takes time.

Warm regards for the holidays,

George

GT/cr

[handwritten annotations]

sc 115/430/74

DHW. 126/off/75/4387

32

(The *Titanic* leaves for her trials, 1 April 1912.)

(In Southampton Water, 10 April 1912.)

TITANIC PROJECT

A NEW biography has been written on the Chatteris man who plans to raise the wreck of a famous British liner.

Ricky Amphlett-Grange, of Victoria Street, Chatteris, has written 'The Not So Ordinary Man of Hong Kong' based on Douglas John Faulkner-Woolley.

Mr Faulkner-Woolley has been interested in the finding and salvaging of the White Star liner, R.M.S Titanic, and many years later, the Cunard liner, R.M.S Queen Elizabeth I.

Whilst studying abroad in a boarding school Mr Amphlett-Grange read about the Titanic and the unfortunate sea disaster. Little did he know that he would one day be involved in a project concerning the same liner.

Mr Amphlett-Grange met Mr Faulkner-Woolley in 1994 and joined the team involved in the Titanic project in July this year.

He said Mr Faulkner-Woolley became very well known in the shipping world due to his salvage methods and plans to raise the wreck of the Titanic, being made known world-wide through press coverage.

The book should be on sale shortly.

33

Lessons of Titanic

THE *TITANIC* was "unsinkable." That is what everybody said. The British passenger liner, the largest and most luxurious ship afloat, had a double-bottomed hull that was divided into 16 watertight compartments. Four of these compartments could be flooded without endangering the great ship's buoyancy, the experts said.

The *Titanic*, however, did sink — on its maiden voyage. It was steaming across the Atlantic Ocean at 22 knots when, shortly before midnight on this date 70 years ago, it struck an iceberg 95 miles south of the Grand Banks of Newfoundland.

The iceberg tore a 300-foot gash in the ship's starboard side and ripped open five of the watertight compartments. At 2:20 the next morning, the *Titanic* sank.

One hour and 20 minutes after that, the liner *Carpathia* arrived and rescued many survivors from the cold sea. But 1,513 of the 2,224 persons aboard the *Titanic* lost their lives.

There was nothing good about the sinking. Some good, however, did come as a result of the sinking. An International Convention for Safety of Life at Sea was convened in 1913, and several safety regulations were established: Every ship must have lifeboat space for each person on board (the *Titanic* had only 1,178 lifeboat spaces). Lifeboat drills must be held during every voyage. All ships at sea must maintain a 24-hour radio watch (the liner *California* was only 20 miles away when the *Titanic* hit the iceberg, but no radioman was on duty aboard the *California* at that late hour).

The sinking also led to establishment of the International Ice Patrol, which warns ships of icebergs in the North Atlantic shipping lanes.

The *Titanic* tragedy is a reminder that even the finest plans go amiss, and that we can learn from such mishaps and do better the next time.

Titanic in glory days   File photo

Steven's Story

When Doug returned to England, from Hong Kong in 1972, he had no money left and had to survive by sleeping rough on the streets of London. Fortunately this was not for long, as it made him more determined to find employment. He found a job in the North of London, working in an engineering factory. This job got him off the streets and into a bedsit in Boundary Road, Edmonton Green. After a while he put his name on the housing list- he remembers getting very frustrated as the local council did not seem to help him much, so he wrote to his local MP, Mr Graham. Within five weeks Doug was given a council flat in Edmonton and that is how he got to know Lord Graham. They became good friends and their friendship is just as strong today as it was in the beginning.

Doug goes on to tell me that one evening he was with a group of people, walking down Boundary Road when they stopped because they had seen a pair of feet sticking out from under a car. It turned out to be a young lad by the name of Steven Bilsby, who at that time was an up coming young artist (some one in the group said that Steven would like to paint one of Doug's model ships on to canvas), but for what ever reasons he decided not to take it up as a full time career. Steven later went to diving school to learn deep sea diving, so as to become part of Doug's team, but he was not long into the course when his instructor left and the new instructor tried to teach a different method, so Steven decided to teach himself and he now is second in command to Doug over his whole project.

Steven did not seem to have a settled home life and he had also spent time in a home. The more that Steven was going round to Doug's, the more reluctant he was to leave, until eventually he ended up sleeping in an old sleeping bag on Doug's floor. Doug eventually became like a father to him.

Doug smiled at me has he told me that he remembered that first glimpse he had of Steven-how much he looked like the character Roofeo from the film 'Hook' and that always tickled Doug. Steven was a sea cadet leading seaman RN, he got CSEs in English and Maths and was reported as 'willing to work.'

(Douglas with Steven)

Extract from Doug's Press Diary:
Diver Steven bids to recover Titanic

The world's most luxurious ocean liner is coming home. After years resting on the sea bed, ambitious plans to raise the wreck of the doomed Titanic are underway.

The remarkable scheme is the brain child of 59-year-old Douglas Woolley, Steven Bilsby's foster father, who claims to have salvage rights to the sunken wreck.

He has registered to claim with Lloyds of London. "It's true and he has registered his right to salvage," said a Lloyds spokesman.

Once recovered, the ship would give Southampton one of the country's leading tourist attractions-if they could fight off opposition from Liverpool for the ship.

But Southampton's leisure boss Councillor Eddie Read in convinced Southampton has stronger links than Liverpool with the "unsinkable" ship.

"Many of the crew came from the city and she sailed from here. We have very strong links and would welcome her back, "he said.

(Steven with diving equipment)
Advertiser OPINION

Titanic ambitions

Some people may scoff when hearing of the daring plans to raise the Titanic and bring it to Southampton as the South's pre-mier tourist attraction. But Lloyds of London are not laughing. They confirm Steven Bilsby's claim of having the sole diving rights to the wreck two miles below the surface. The plans are brave, imagnative and adventurous, in the great tradition of Britain's explorers reaching back to Raleigh, Drake and beyond.

If this dream comes true, the future prosperity of the city as a tourist attraction is assured for the next century. It will become Southampton's Buckingham Place and Tower Bridge rolled into one.

And if people mock the idea, let them. They were probably as dismissive when it was proposed that the Tudor warship the Mary Rose be raised from the seas that had engulfed it for hundreds of years. But there remains one serious and sensitive issue that must take priority over any commercial consideration.

Before a second thought is given to this scheme, it must first be determined how the remains of those who perished in the disaster be ultimately laid to rest with the dignity they are due.

This will be done.

This is Steven's story.

Steven at sea.

RS & COMMISSIONERS FOR OATHS

SATURDAY MORNING BY
APPOINTMENT ONLY

PARTNERS
J. C. LINDSELL

ASSISTANT SOLICITOR:
D. WALMSLEY

I/We certify that a true copy of this notice
was served upon the

Solicitors on the   day of

                19   .

.LAS JOHN FAULKNER-WOOLLEY
QE1 and TITANIC Salvage Project
Signed _Salvors and Seawise Salvage CO.s_
Jersey C.I.
U.K.   BRITISH HONG KONG
Solicitor for the

19   .—No.

IN THE COURT OF APPEAL
On Appeal from

*The Supreme Court
of Hong Kong.*

SC 115/436/74
SC 500/5/13-111

Plaintiff

Defendant

Ownership

In order to get ownership of the Titanic contract, Mr Woolley set about contacting everyone who had a claim on the ship.

"I got them to waive their claims and then I put notices in national newspaper about my claim. No-one challenged it and I have been told this will stand up in court," he said.

But Mr Woolley's plans have been thwarted over his attempts to raise another ship, the Queen Elizabeth I, which lies in Hong Kong harbour.

It was meant as a pilot scheme to attract backers for the Titanic project, but legal wrangles have caused costly delays.

Mr Woolley remains optimistic: "I have been working on this stage for the last four years and it looks very promising.

I hope the court problems will be sorted out by July and I have got a dead-line of five years to complete the operation.

The bold venture is not all about making money though, because it is also Mr Woolley's intention to feature the two ships in a maritime museum.

His claims have been backed by Mr Tony Wakefield, a salvage expert and consulting engineer who will get the contract to raise the Titanic should the scheme come to fruition.

"He certainly has a case and a sporting chance of pulling it off. I would say it was just possible he can do it," Mr Wakefield said.

2-4-1991,

Titanic struggle to reach for dream

By Ken Elkes

To say Doug Woolley has faced a "titanic" struggle in reaching for his life-long dream would not be an understatement.

In fact, for someone who claims he owns the contract to raise the Titanic itself and plans to do it within five years, it is very appropriate.

The 56-year-old former Shropshire man is currently looking for backers for his £15 million project, which he hopes will make him into a multi-millionaire.

Mr Woolley, who now lives and works in London, first became interested in the massive ship — sunk by an iceberg on its maiden voyage in 1911 — during his childhood in Worthen, near Shrewsbury.

Mr Woolley's grandfather, a grave-digger at Worthen Church, used to recount the tale of his sister who booked a passage to America on the great ship.

As she stood on the dockside she had a premonition of disaster and refused to board the ill-fated ship, which went down taking more than 1,000 lives.

"I started to get the idea of retrieving her lost property which had already been put on the ship — that was the spark which began all of it," said Mr Woolley.

He developed an interest in science at school and later came up with an idea of using petroleum jelly, which is lighter than water, to raise the ship.

DOUGLAS JOHN FAULKNER-WOOLLEY
QE1 and TITANIC Salvage Project
Salvors and Seawise Salvage CO.s
Jersey C.I.
U.K.   BRITISH HONG KONG
Agent for

of

,Solicitor.

(Look-out Frederick Fleet [front row 'circled'] was the first to see the iceberg. Shown here with other crew members after the disaster.)

V, a real-life eration to se the Titanic

All lights blazing . . . how she went down

By Geoffrey Levy

he says "So even if the whole thing fails, they can cut their losses.

"On the face of it, it seems to be a fairly speculative thing. But if it's a success, the backers could double their money."

The most likely method of raising the ship is rather different from that used in Clive Cussler's novel which the Express has been serialising

In the book the gaping holes in the liner's hull are sealed before the vessel is filled with air pumped in at terrific pressure.

As it then floats upwards valves adjust the pressure so that the hull does not burst.

In real life, oil filled nylon bags will probably be used to attempt the lift. Using deep-sea diving equipment like the bathyscaphe, which descended almost two miles to the sunken American submarine Scorpion some years ago, the salvage team will deposit the bags inside the hull.

They will then be pumped

full of oil (four-fifths the weight of water) until the ship is buoyant Theoretically, the 882ft long vessel should then rise to the surface.

The Titanic sank on her maiden voyage on April 15, 1912, when she struck a monster iceberg at 22 knots 400 lies south-east of Newfoundland.

The band played on as she sank. Out of 2,207 passengers and crew, 1,502 perished.

Gold on board

For the last 25 years Douglas Woolley, sometime factory worker and telephonist and now living in North London, has been planning to recover her.

He has probably read every word ever written in English about the tragedy, met survivors, gathered a team of enthusiasts and salvage experts about him and formed the Titanic Salvage Company.

But until now it has been

25 years of frustration. Nobody was really interested in risking the money, even though Woolley believes there is gold and silver worth £80 million on board.

This time it was the potential source of finance which approached 42-year-old Woolley, rather than the other way about. He immediately sought the help of his City acquaintance, Philip Slade, whose role has been that of "middleman."

It is no five-minute project. First there will be a thorough survey which will take around sixmonths. "There is quite a weather problem to contend with in that part of the world," says Slade.

He estimates that from the word go the project will take at least three years, possibly five.

Hearty laughter

The operation would be run from West Germany. "The company will be set up in West Berlin to take advantage of their tax laws," he says.

Douglas Woolley's pre-occupation with the most famous maritime catastrophe in history have led many people to label him a crank.

His obsession scheme to raise the Titanic has caused hearty laughter in some maritime, technical and financial circles.

A few guffaws have even come from Lloyd's, who underwrote the original Commercial Union policy on the hull and paid out £1 million as a result.

Commercial Union has never yielded its interest in the sunken ship.

But if the Titanic really does contain the treasures Woolley believes, the feeling in insurance circles yesterday was that it would be too difficult now for individuals to make claims. "Woolley and his friends would have a pretty clear run," said a Lloyd's man.

Douglas Woolley may have the last laugh yet.

Mr C. H. BETTS

Doug started to trust me more, and told me how he had first got interested in the Titanic and explained about that contract as well as the companies that were formed after the contract, such as Salvors which was formed on 4th May 1972 in Jersey and the Directors were Mr B. Hamilton, Mr S. Kingsley and Mr M. Forrest.Then there was Seawise & Titanic Salvage Ltd on 14th November 1977 whose directors were
Mr P. Slade, Mr C, Ramsay, Mr J. Wilkins, plus a public relation person by the name of Mr D. Berwin. There were also about 83 more smaller companies that were also owned by those named above. It appeared that through these companies Mr J. Grimm became involved via Mr P. Slade and Mr B.Tantum.

This reminds me of another story Doug told me about Mr J. Grimm's involvement with Slade and a Mr F. Leuchter, who is an American. Leuchter made the plans to salvage the Titanic with the backing of Mr Grimm in 1987. He brought Doug in to his deal as Doug was, and still is, the only person to have an existing claim to salvage the Titanic. Leuchter stated ' in something like this, the best position to be in is to be in bed with the people who have the claim." There were a number of problems and according to Leuchter, Doug and Mr Grimm " had a sort of falling out" over some kind of dispute, but Mr Grimm saw things in a different way. Mr Grimm stated, " I am not and never have been involved with a Mr Leuchter." As for the falling out between Doug and Mr Grimm there has never been one, because they have never dealt with each other directly, only through Slade. A good friend of Doug's, Charlie Betts, became very annoyed with what he saw as a failure on Leuchter placed an artical in The Times of London, that Woolley and Leuchter entered into contract with Mr Grimm- that was untrue.

I asked Charlie to tell me a bit about himself and his involvement with Doug. Over the years people have seen the raising of the Titanic and QE1 as being an impossible task, but " they could not be more wrong" he said. Charlie remembers that Doug, Steven and himself were invited on to a Frank Carson's chat show and he told Frank, when asked about raising of the Titanic, "nothing was impossible."

Mr Charlie Betts

40

Charlie goes on to say he has been telling Doug for twenty odd years never to give up, despite all the knock backs that he might encounter, and that he would always be there to help him.

I asked him what was his opinion of Dr Ballard stating that he was the first to locate where the Titanic was resting,and his reply to that was that Doug had found the location years before it was ever reported by Dr Ballard. This can be proved as Doug has always kept records of anything and everything concerning the Titanic. This information was used for their own gain and they made plenty out of it. They may think they are off the hook, but Doug does not give up that easily-he will see it through to the end, with the help of his good friends.

Charlie said that he can't name names, that is up to Doug, but he said that he has had some dealing with these people and they are only out for what they can get, like the people who dealt with Doug in 1972 (some may remember the meeting at Bishopsgate.)

Some years ago a Mr Leuchter, of Boston USA, contacted Doug in connection with plans to raise the Titanic. He said that he was a close friend of Mr Jack Grimm of the First National Bank, USA. Doug 'phoned Mr Grimm who was a bit offensive, to which Doug answered that "there was no reason to be rude just because you are a millionaire." Mr Grimm apologised and went on to say that he did not know a Mr Leuchter . This was also reported by Mr Grimm in the press in Boston (and by Chalie).

Charlie said that he once met a Miss Kean whose father was lost on the Titanic. His job was to look after all jewellery. This lady was 80 years old and still doing work for the RWVS. Charlie met her at a sale of Titanic mementos while he was with Doug and Steven and he said that Doug was treated like a lord by Miss Kean and that she fully backs what Doug is trying to do.

Charlie ended his story by stating that the truth will rise to the surface and that anyone who has read this book and still disbelieves in Doug, then they should read it again and then find the proof in documents provided.

Doug had moved from London now and I was helping him more and more. As the letters to courts were becoming the thing of the moment it was like the blind leading the blind, but we did it. I remember suggesting that he needed a public Relations person to try sell his story to the papers. Doug agreed and we looked through the Yellow Pages and found one who lived in St Ives, Huntingdon. Doug sat down and composed a letter , telling him a little bit about his quest. A couple of days went by and Doug received a letter back from Mr Roddis saying that he would be interested in helping and arranged to meet Doug at his home.Doug asked me if I would like to be in on the meeting and I said that I would. On the face of it the first meeting with Mr Roddis seemed very promising. Also from the first meeting it was decided that a formal contract between Doug and Mr Roddis be made and agreed with the utmost urgency.

Other things discussed at that first meeting were.

1. What qualifications he had in this line of work? His reply was that he had not done anything like this before, but had written two books on the famous Brooklands Race track as well as helping to save it.

2. He is also currently doing a biography on John Major MP.

A few days later I had to go to the local library to look up something about the two ships, and remembered the two books Peter had said that he had written. I could not find them on the shelves so I asked one of the librarians if they could tell me of any books by the author Peter Roddis . They looked on their computer and told me that they had no books by that author. Also at that first meeting he told Doug that he would write a letter to the Governor of Hong Kong and also to the Prime Minister. At the second meeting he brought along with him a four page contract for Doug to sign. After all the signing was finished, I asked Peter, if his books were under different names, they could not be found in the library and Doug confirmed it.

In this contract some of the things he would do are as follows:

1. He would write all court letters and documents and show them to Doug before sending them.

2. Sell the story to the media for as much as he could.

3. To do all this in Doug's best interest.

Going back to number 1, he did manage to send one very important letter to the Supreme Court in Hong Kong without Doug's consent, and when he showed Doug a copy it was noted that he had put in one little word that could have cost Doug everything. That little word was PART. What the word should have been was ALL OR IN TOTAL, as per the order of justice. A complete copy of that letter is as follows:

12th April 1995

Mr J. R. Robins
Legal aid department , Hong Kong and copy to Supreme Court Hong Kong.

Dear Mr Robins,

Legal aid application- Mr D. J. Woolley

Enforcement of salvage contract on H.K.

I refer to your letter on the 17/3/1995 addressed to Mr D.J.W. in which you advice him that his legal aid appeal is adjourned until the 10/5/1995 to enable me to prepare representations on his behalf.

On Mr Woolley's instructions brief I have drawn up on his behalf the enclosed statement together with copies of documents from Mr Woolley's files which so that in good faith he entered into a contract with Messrs Hamilton, Kingsley and others, who at the time represented bona fide companies, in a bid to salvage the wreck of the ship Seawise University, formerly known as the QE1 in H.K. and that contract was breached. This part of a quite complicated matter that has been dragged out for many years involves other aspects which I believe are not relevant for the purposes of this appeal. Accordingly I have made this representation as simple as possible. Mr Woolley's complaint does stem from this breach of contract and he in many ways suffered significant losses and injury as a result of this over the ensuing years. It is vital for Mr Woolley to gain judgement in this matter if he is to obtain satisfaction of the other associated matters, which are outside the justification of the Supreme Court Hong Kong.

It is unfortunate that the losses Mr Woolley has suffered as the result of this breach of contract have direct bearing on the impecunious state he has found himself in over several years, as he has been obliged to represent himself without any experience in legal matter, nor any knowledge of the procedures.

Many people including members of the House of Lords and the Parliament of the states of Jersey, C.I. have suggested that with proper legal advice and representation, Mr Woolley would have been justified in the matter of this breach of contract some years ago. He must now rely on the legal aid department for assistance to have any chance of recouping some part of the losses and injury he has suffered for many years.

Yours sincerely

P. Roddis

Apart from the word part there were two other mistake that he made. They were "bona fide companies"- Salvors was formed after the contract was made, and his other mistake was that he made his opinion of what was and was not important.

We then found that any suggestions made by either myself or Doug were completely ignored, so much that Doug had to phone him and remind him of his contract. His reply to this way by letter, Doug that if he thought that he was not doing the job, then he would pull out. This happened a couple of times before Doug finally gave him the easy way out- and that was when I told Doug that I would try and write the book for him.

He introduced me to some of his important friends by getting me to write a letter to them, explaining who I was, and Doug had asked me to write to get some information out of them about Doug and he would put a little note inside to say it was alright. That was to people like LORD GRAHAM OF EDMONTON and SENATOR LE MAIN OF JERSEY whom I have corresponded with on a number of occasions, by letter, since that first time.

(Senator Le Main)

Bill Tantum also set up a company with Dr Ballard called Seaonics Inc. This company was formed with the express intention of salvaging the Titanic after doing a survey. Ballard worked for 'Wood's Hole'. It was said that they used an undersea sub called Alvin to do that survey. Mr Tantum claimed that they found the Titanic, but Dr J. Ewing of Wood's Hole was contracted and the truth was established, that Alvin had never been used on a Titanic venture and this throws doubt on later surveys.

Lord Graham wrote a letter to Baroness Dunn in Hong Kong to ask her if there was any thing that she could do to help Doug. Her response was that we should contact her aide in London. I also wrote a letter to a Mr Wakefield, whom I have never received a reply from.

Apart from writing this book, I am also involved in doing some video work with my friend Graham Mead. It was through my perseverance in writing this book that finally made him become interested in the project and we are making video accounts of interviews with Doug in the hope that a television company will be interested in buying them. Between Graham and myself, if Doug wants to go anywhere then we take him. Graham has taken Doug up to Liverpool to visit Doug's mother and sister, and I have taken him back to Shropshire so that he can trace his family tree (see 'The Family Tree'). It is very important to him where comes from; he can trace his family back to the Cadwallardrs who are of Royal Decree, as that was the name of the last King of Wales and Doug is very proud that he is part of that family.

When we have been to Shropshire, I have met some of his family. I've met auntie

Dot, Uncle Thom and his wife, and a cousin who is also interested in compiling the family tree, and when we were there Doug compared notes. They all have their own little stories to tell and they all seem to be very proud their heritage.

Uncle Thom told me about a chair that was given to a member of the family by Queen Victoria, for a long and loyal service as her solicitor. Thom is proud of that chair. Pop's had an auntie who was a lady-in-waiting to Queen Victoria.

(The chair given by Queen Victoria)

There was a time when Pops was in hospital and he sent a photo of three men on the deck of a salvage ship and one of the men in the picture was circled along with the photo was a brief letter that referred to the picture and said that the man which was circled was his grandson, Doug and that the three men had just died in a ship accident. Who sent the letter and picture no one knows, but the only people who would have a photo like that would be the people who made contract in 1972.

It was only a few weeks after this shock that pops passed on.

Titanic treasure sought on wreck

WEST BERLIN (Reuter) — A fabulous treasure is believed to be still aboard the wreck of the liner *Titanic* on the floor of the Atlantic Ocean and a group of West Berlin businessmen have launched a project to salvage it.

The glittering prize is pouches of diamonds with an estimated value, the businessmen say, of $212.5 million.

The three businessmen sponsoring the project, launched 65 years after the *Titanic* sank with the loss of 1,513 lives, say it is well advanced.

One of them, Thomas Gfroerer, 28, said investors would soon be asked to sign up for minimum stakes of $2,125, with a possible profit of up to 500 per cent.

"We are sure we'll be able to raise the $21.5 million needed for the whole operation on the German capital market," he said, adding that investors would get 85 per cent of their money back in case of failure."

Journalist W. T. Stead one of the many who drowned, had published a strangely prophetic story a few years earlier about a similar tragedy

Steven R.N and Friends

45

WYCHBOLD CHURCH CHOIR QUARTET.
WINNERS OF A CUP AT THE CHELTENHAM MUSIC FESTIVAL. 1913.
BILL COLLEY, FRED WINTER, STEVE STRIDE, TOM AMPHLETT.

(On the afternoon of 15 April the only bad news on the front page was that Christy Mathewson had lost his first start of the season.)

47

1. Mr Bruce Ismay, Chairman of the White Star Line
2. Major A. Peuchen, of the Canadian Rifles
3. Major A.W. Butt, Aide-de-camp to President Taft
4. Mr C.M. Hays, President of the Grand Trunk Railway
5. Mrs J.J. Astor
6. Colonel J.J. Astor, the multi-millionaire
7. Lady Cosmo Duff-Gordon (known as "Lucile"), wife of Sir Cosmo Duff-Gordon, BT
8. Mr Jack Phillips, wireless operator on the *Titanic*
9. The Countess of Rothes
10. Mr Daniel Marvin, son of the head of a great American cinematograph firm
11. Mrs Daniel Marvin
12. Mr W.T. Stead, the distinguished journalist
13. Mr Benjamin Guggenhein, a well known American Can banker and multi-millionaire
14. Mr Karl H. Behr, the lawn-tennis player
15. Mr Isidor Straus, a member of congress and a multi-millionaire banker

Into the harbour bed.

He still intends to pursue his rights to the salvage and return of the seawise which are subject to a contract of salvage. What is particularly intriguing are the lenths that others have gone to, to prevent him making his claim.
Apart from the burglary on his apartment, My friend has been threatened, attacked and put in hospital and abducted in bang kok to prevent him from getting to Hong Kong to make inquiries as to how the contract was going, He believes this may be because the raising of the wreck could reveal evidence connected with it's mysterious end, He dose have documentary evidence to support that the contract dose exist and still remains valid.

My friend is a quite ordinary man who has extraordinary experiences to relate, He still has a great deal of documentary evidence to support his claims . He has quite simply been trying to gather support for his aspirations, Without knowing how to make himself heard in the right quarters.

There must be the making of an extremely adventurous and intriguing story here and he agrees to tell it in order to raise sufficient funds to enable him to appoint professional legal representatives to pursue his case on a properly based footing. The story would include his views and observations on some of the claims about artefacts that have been recovered from the Titanic, which he says are dubious, and other background on the British flagships.

He has appointed me to handle this on his behalf, I am making this an open letter to the media and the story will go to the highest bidder. I would appreciate a response as soon as possible, I can provide much more details on interest.

CLIVE AMPHLETT

YOURS SINCERELY

IFT PLAN

GO AL

By MALCOLM BROMHALL

Ilford man Douglas Woolley has been given the go-ahead for his scheme to raise the liner Queen Elizabeth.

And Mr Woolley—who sees the plan as a giant dress rehearsal for his bid to raise the Titanic—says the operation should be under way in less than eight weeks.

"This is a marvellous chance," he told the Comet this week.

"At last we are beginning to become recognised.

"I wrote to the ship's owner—millionaire Mr C. Y. Tung—and I have received a letter back saying we can have the chance.

"He has asked us to submit detailed plans.

"We are delighted. It will be the dress rehearsal for the big job later this year."

The notion of raising the Titanic was inspired by his grandfather. "He told me about an aunt who had booked a trip on the maiden voyage but cancelled her ticket because she had a premonition of disaster."

● Douglas Woolley . . . another sea adventure

"I was pressed into service on the railway," he says. "I was passing the station one day when the stationmaster called me over and gave me a note to take to the signalbox up the line. When I got there I found that the note was a letter of appoinment. I was the new signalman."

The embryonic idea had plenty of time to flourish and mature in the solitude of the 12 years that followed: the fact of his unsuitability for factory life took only a month or so to become apparent, and he left immediately for Shropshire, where he was first farm-worker and later a railway signalman.

President: D.J. Woolley   Consultants: Salvors Ltd.

49

CONTRACT NOTE CHARLTON SEAL SCHAVERIEN LIM[ITED]

P.O. Box 512, 76 Cross Street, Manchester M60 2EP Telephone: 061-8
Telex: 666894 CSDCOG. Fax: 061-832 9092.

London Office:
18½ Seklorde Street, London EC1R 0HN
Telephone: 01-251 1626. Telex: 262120. Fax: 01-251 3983

VAT No. 494 6326 15
Registered in England No. 211 3603
Registered Address: Henrietta House, 9 Henrietta Place, London W1M 9AG
Member of The International Stock Exchange and The Securities Associati[on]
A Benchmark Group Company

WE HAVE SOLD FOR SEAWI0001 AS AGENTS
Account Number

SEAWISE & TITANIC SALVAGE LIMITED

Bargain Date & Tax Point   04 JAN 198? for settlement   11 JAN 1989
Reference   BMS00194   SECURITY 2252285

15:00   2000   DALLAS ENVIRON'HEALTH'SYSTEMS $0.02 $30.00
                 COM STK NPV   SS

CHARGES BASED ON $ 10 £1 =1.82

THIS SECURITY IS NOT OFFICIALLY LISTED ON THE UK STOCK EXC[HANGE]

CHARLTON SEAL SCHAVERIEN LTD

SUBJECT TO THE RULES AND REGULATIONS OF THE STOCK EXCHANGE INCLUDING ANY
TEMPORARY REGULATIONS MADE BY OR UNDER IT
AND SUBJECT TO THE TERMS & CONDITIONS OF THE ...TY OF THE COUNCIL

£1

$30.00

£1:

£1

AACM[S]

[handwritten notes]
Wireless File S.S.S.C.
(3 - Nerus) C.M. RAMSAY FSSC cryptt
agree to use on Marsden JW
Titanic and Seawise Salvage Again
and engrais to the Clearing and
Titles off No. Discrepts.
sig C.M. Ramsay
Date 27 Sept 1975

"I should end Mr Ramsay
from Point of the Salvage team.
But Dewey was sold out big

There on Discretio of STS (?)
should be in accordance to the
Mods 14 Nov - 1972 ...
Homilton - managers
whose of scheme ...) of Seawise ...
... G.E.(?) of Hong Kong.

Hungarian Method to be Used by Three-nation Team

BUDAPEST, Wednesday

A three-nation team will try in December to salve the British passenger liner *Titanic*, which sank after hitting a North Atlantic iceberg in 1912, a Hungarian news agency has reported. The agency said a team of seven Britons, one Austrian and two Hungarians would use a newly-developed Hungarian process in their

ISE THE TANIC

The doomed Titanic in Southampton three days before tragedy overtook her. Photo courtesy of Patrick Stephens Publishing.

"Echo" Shipping Reporter

DOUGLAS WOOLLEY, the former factory worker whose ambition is to raise the ex-Queen Elizabeth in Hong Kong harbour and the wreck of the Titanic in the Atlantic, says he has received telephone calls threatening his life.

And Mr. Woolley has revealed that when he returned from a trip to Hong Kong at Christmas two men entered his London flat and beat him up. He says he was taken to hospital with severe bruising and injuries to his face, legs and arms.

Since then he says he has received two threatening telephone calls, by "a man with a very deep voice." He has told the police and they are visiting his home regularly, says Mr. Woolley.

"The first 'phone call warned me that I would get a bullet in my head if I did not give up my project," Mr. Woolley told me. The latest call also threatened his life if he did not drop his salvage ideas.

"When I got the first threat I passed it over as a sick joke, but it's a bit more serious now."

Mr. Woolley does not intend to drop his plans. At present he is in dispute with the Channel Islands salvage company Salvors Ltd., over what he alleges were contracts connected with the raising of the ex-Queen Elizabeth.

Salvors deny that contracts exist, claiming that they only issued letters of intent.

Diver Steven bids to recover £88m sunken treasure

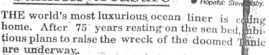

By Suzanne Dixon

THE world's most luxurious ocean liner is coming home. After 75 years resting on the sea bed, ambitious plans to raise the wreck of the doomed Titanic are underway.

Southampton diver Steven Bilsby is planning to raise the ruin a £13m bid to recover sunken treasure totalling £88m. The salvage operation will set sail from Ocean Village late next month for a 3,500 mile trip and, if successful, the ocean going vessel and treasure she will be berthed in Southampton's dock.

The remarkable scheme is the brainchild of 52-year-old Douglas Woolley, Stephen Bilsby's foster father, who claims to have the salvage rights to the sunken wreck.

He has registered the claim with Lloyds of London. "It's true he has been claiming this for 20 years and he has registered his right to salvage," said a Lloyds spokesman.

Together with American millionaire Jack Grim the couple plan to "take possession" of the wreck on Wednesday, April 15 — the 75th anniversary of its sinking.

They hope extensive survey work will pinpoint the mass of jewels, diamonds and gold rumoured to be aboard in a six month blitz on the boat before an operation to raise the vessel, due to begin 12 months later.

The diamonds are thought to rest in the bow of the White Star ship that went down on her maiden voyage with the loss of 1,513 lives. But the aft section would be recovered too when the broken-backed liner is brought to the surface.

Special electronic equipment would be used to recover most of the haul from the wreck, settled two and a half miles down on the Atlantic ocean bed.

Once recovered, the ship would give Southampton one of the country's leading tourist attractions — if they could fight off opposition from Liverpool for the boat.

As builders of the liner that city would want her too and the salvage team are convinced there would be a fight to get the boat.

But Southampton's Leisure boss Coun. Eddie Read is convinced Southampton has stronger links than Liverpool with the "unsinkable" boat.

"Many of the crew came from the city and she sailed from here. We have very strong links and would welcome her back," he said.

Titanic mission

UNEMPLOYED Aspley man Philip Roberts has landed a prize place in the salvage squad which plans to raise the Titanic.

He will be part of a top team headed Titanic expert Douglas Woolley, who has been trying to retrieve the "unsinkable" liner for more than a quarter of a century.

Mr Roberts reckons £6m funding has almost been raised and that the incredible quest to refloat the world's most famous ship wreck will begin next spring.

"I've only been involved with the project for about a year, but Mr Woolley has been trying to raise the Titanic for 27 years," he explained.

22309205

On the verge of the 'impossible' dream

OUR MISSION—TO RAISE THE TITANIC!

- Could it really happen? The Titanic breaks the surface in a dramatic scene from *the film Rai...*

News feature by ROGER FULTON

GROUP of men are taking up one of the greatest challenges in sea history —to raise the Titanic from the clutches of Davy Jones' locker.

It sounds like a "mission impossible," dreamed by the group of over-optimistic fanatics, but the men behind the venture insist : "We are not cranks, we really mean it. This is going to be one of the greatest adventures of all time."

The bait is indeed enormous — at least £80 million worth of gold, priceless art treasures, including an 8th century copy of The Rubaiyat by Omar Khayam, as well as a fortune in world film and story rights.

The full scope of the project was revealed last week at a meeting, in the Museum Lane Community Centre, Boreamwood, of Seaproit Ltd, the company set up to deal with the salvage.

On Wednesday, 69 years to the day, since the Titanic sank on April 15, 1912, company chairman Doug Woolley announced that after years of painstaking research and planning, they were now on the verge of a multi-million pound deal to bring the ship and its cargo back to the surface.

Mr Woolley, a 44 year-old freelance engineer, who sees he has established himself as sole legal claimant to the salvage of the wreck, said that if the financial negotiations go through, the first stage of the scheme—a full survey...

Boreamwood, Mr Gurr has spent ten years reading and researching every scrap of information he could find about the Titanic, piecing together the clues until he is now certain he has found the liner's exact location — 2½ miles down in an area of 28 square miles, some 430 miles south east of Newfoundland.

The two met, fatefully, at a showing of A Night To Remember—the original film version of the disaster when 1,500 people died after the Titanic hit an...

...such as sonar ... photon ... magnetometer ... ch detects ... differences in the earth's ...

...treated using a similar process to the methods of protecting North Sea oil...

R.J. Amphlett

Doug and R.J.Amphlett at Hadzor

Nasrallahs: Nicola

Three of the men who plan to raise the Titanic (left to right) Doug Woolley, Dennis Bissett and Ian Gurr.

The ships wireless was made by Marconi Co Ltd now at Chelmsford. It was the very best. It had multiple tuner. It was the pre-courser of the modern T.V and computer and the floppy disk.

First class promenade deck may be as seen by FR. Browne. RC.

First class State Room it had marble wash Basin and Showers they were of the Highest Order.

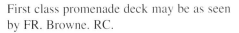

OF AMPHLETT

Family fortunes in
words and pictures

Talk of the Devil has revealed the story of a family connection with Wychbold spanning 120 years.

This week we can show you a unique view of the idyllic link between the Amphlett family and Wychbold Hall at the turn of the century.

The Amphlett and Wychbold Hall connection began in the 1830s when Richard Paul Amphlett bought the site of New Hall or Wychbold Hall.

There he built a new hall which was later inherited by his nephew, Richard Hamden Amphlett, and his wife, Sophia.

Great War

Judge Amphlett died in 1925 but his wife Sophia — whose grandfather, Dr Phillip Gibbs, had been private physician to Czar Nicholas II of Russia — continued to live at the original hall until 1936.

By then her own heir, Richard Ferrand Amphlett, had been killed in the Great War, so the hall was left to the Rev Richard John Marshall Amphlett.

He decided because of subsidence on the original site to build a new hall nearby.

The new hall was smaller but just as grand.

But sadly, since the Amphlett family left in the 1950s, it has become the haunt of vandals and a target for the elements.

Thankfully, the hall is to be saved by Midland developers who will soon begin to restore it to a luxury hotel.

ABOVE: Richard Ferrand Amphlett, son of Judge Amplett.

He married Mary Blackford Marshall, an American woman who was a descendant of the fourth Chief Justice of the United States.

He served in the Great War, where he was killed in action, and his children included the Rev Richard John Marshall Amphlett, who died after preaching a sermon in Birmingham in 1978, and Mary, who still lives in Worcester.

LEFT: Two members of the Amphlett family standing by Wychbold Hall.

The QE.1 Story :

Claim relates to the old QE liner

"Echo" Shipping Reporter

MR. DOUGLAS WOOLLEY, the ex-factory worker whose life ambition is to raise the wreck of the White Star liner Titanic from her Atlantic grave, claims that a Jersey-based salvage company have broken their contract with his company.

The contract obligations Mr. Woolley claims from Salvors Ltd., of St. Helier, were in connection with another wreck — that of the ex-Cunard flagship Queen Elizabeth which caught fire and sank in Hong Kong harbour while being refitted by shipowner Mr. C. Y. Tung as the Seawise University.

In lawyers' hands

But a spokesman for Salvors told me yesterday: "I know of no such contract." He said Mr. Woolley had been warned that he would not be allowed to consume the letters and address of Salvors on the note paper of Mr. Woolley's Titanic Salvage Company and the Seawise Salvage Company.

But the spokesman refused to discuss the matter of the alleged contract any further. "It is in the hands of our lawyers," he said.

Mr. Woolley claims that a letter from Salvors' managing director, Mr. Brian Hamilton, dated April 29, 1972, accepted the terms of a contract which involved a retaining fee of £30,000.

MR. Douglas Woolley with the hulk of the Seawise behind him.

'Letters of intent'

At about that time, a spokesman for the company told the "Echo" that Salvors had instigated a survey of the Queen Elizabeth in Hong Kong on their own behalf, and that their link with Mr. Woolley's companies depended upon guarantees of finance. They confirmed the existence only of 'letters of intent.'

Mr. Woolley, who has spent all his savings on his project, including a proposed visit to Hong Kong itself, is now demanding £7,000 compensation for contract severance from Salvors, or the carrying out of what he claims are their contractual obligations.

57

Court Matter
Hong Kong and Jersey

The plaintiff did not discover and could not have discovered without the letter of government records service 13/12/1994 Hong Kong. I now ask for these documents to be placed before the Supreme Court of Hong Kong and enter this as new grounds for my application for Legal Aid and to put my case under exclusion of time limit for my action in the matter of concealment and the enforcement of the QE1 salvage contract.

The Court are subject to various exceptions, such as notice must be given to defence of limitation (re: action out of time) and that facts have been concealed from the Court, ref. My letter 11/6/1995 registrar of the Court stated if however you believe you have new grounds to put forward then the course for you to adopt is to make application to Director of Legal Aid, this is now being done. I'm now asking for the documents held by the Hong Kong government to be placed before the Courts alongside the documents laid before the Court 15/3/1995 and 10/5/1995 and the remonstrance as filed before. I feel there has been a breach of duty by those named by the act of concealment. the defence cannot afford no defence of concealment.This now gives me right of action enforcement of the salvage contract. My present situation is that I remain unemployed and have zero in my bank account as prior records show.

Signed D.J. Woolley

The QE1 mystery

The QE1 must be out of Hong Kong by June 1997. As from now Doug is vetting all members. The sort of people Doug is looking for are to be able to keep the strictest confidence in all that they do concerning the project, able to work in a team and also use their own initiative.This team is being brought together to meet the challenge of the 1972 contract. It is not just about underwater divers, but about the whole shooting match from start to finish, and all falls on the shoulders of those chosen to manage the various tasks.

The QE1 was officially named and launched on the 27th September 1938 by Queen Elizabeth, now the Queen Mother. She said at the time that she was the noblest ship ever to have been built. It seems that the QE1 ended her life with the same secrets as when her life begun. The government at the time was feeding the Germans with a lot of propaganda and the plan was so intense that they even sent great crates of ships fittings and provisions to Southampton. Also word was leaked out that they had reserved the George V dry dock for inspection of the QE1's hull. They did this by getting a crew together and sending them to Southampton ready to take control of her when she had finished her sea trials; They paid for the crew to stay in hotel accommodation and the Germans must have believed the story.

But she never got to Southampton- she went straight to America to start moving troops into place. She was carrying about 15,000+troops per trip and it was said that the two Queens cut two years off the end of the war.

When QE1 left the Clyde, she left under the name HM Troop ship162. She was in a semi-finished state and it was decided that she was too much of a target if she was to stay any length of time in her fitting-out berth. The Admiralty wanted to get the QE1 moved on so as to get the warships ready.

With the QE1's crew waiting for her at Southampton the Admiralty recruited the crew of the Aquitania under the command of Captain John Townley. One of his officers during those war years was an American by the name of Lt John Parker RMVR of Boston Massachusetts. He became one of the finest US countrymen to be part of the Royal Navy. The ship headed straight for New York without any regular trials of her machinery.

It was Sir Winston Churchill, who was at that time the First Lord of Admiralty, that personally made the decision to save her. On 2nd November the Ministry of Shipping gave the orders to rush the completion or make her ready to be at least seaworthy.

On 26th February the QE1 was gently taken out of her fitting-out basin and the Duke of York put her in place. Then on 2nd March 1940 the QE1 crept through the anti-submarine nets at the mouth of the River Clyde and joined the main stream of the sea for her first journey, not as one of Curard's best ships, but as a navy vessel in drab navy grey.

Yes, Britain was at war, but when Queen Mary first left the Clyde in May 1936, she was caught by a gust of wind that blew her into the narrow channel and made her run aground. They decided not to take ant chances with the QE1, so they took off all her lifeboats to make her as light as possible, before towing her up the Clyde to a place called The Tail of the Bank. This is where she dropped anchor for the first time. Now that she was in deeper water she was able to take her lifeboats back on board and they could start to do the final checks while the Captain waited for his orders to arrive via the King's messenger.

It was a very cold, dark night and very quite, but that silence was soon broken by the noise of launch approaching the still and quite QE1. The launch came alongside and the King's messenger boarded the ship and gave Captain Townley his orders. The British waters were infested with German U-boats but the 1,031ft QE1 managed to get past.

There was another problem. The German battleship Deutschland was known to be off the Hebrides and it would have been a great blow to the British morale if the greatest liner of all was sunk before commencing war duty. But with luck or God on her side she came through unblemished. Once the QE1 had reached New York she was fitted out so as to cope with long sea duties, but had no troop accommodation.

She sailed to Singapore where she was fitted for service as a troop transporter. It seemed that the U-boats were not the biggest problem the QE1 had to face in the

Indian Ocean but the heat, as the QE1 was built to keep its passengers cosy in the chilly north Atlantic. The QE1 did not have air -conditioning and on one trip, when she was bound for the Suez in the dead of summer in 1941, the severe problem of heat nearly caused a mutiny, as fights were breaking out all over the ship and were only made quite when a cook was stuffed into a still hot oven and was nearly roasted alive. This action seemed to sober up minds of the troops and peace was restored.

In April 1941 she joined her sister ship conveying Australian troops to the Middle East where the desert war was in full swing. Then, ready for her role in carrying troops from Australia and America to wherever they were needed, the two Queens carried 1,577,000 service personnel during their was service and did this without losing one single life.

Sir Winston Churchill stated that two Queens had shortened the war in Europe by at least a year and continued: "To those who brouhgt these two great ships into existence, the world owes a debt that will not be easy to measure".

In 1941 America entered into the war but Australians and New Zealanders who had been shipped out to the North African front felt endangered by the Japanese as they were pushing through the South Pacific islands. In months that followed, the two Queens were very busy taking American troops to Australia. After the first voyage they had to ban the chewing of gum as it took an army of cleaners and scrapers to clean the decks of the remains.

Another problem was the on each trip they had to carry 500,000 bottles of soda which meant that they would have as many empty bottles to unload at the other end. On one occasion, because of the shortage of glass, they had to count all the empties and could only account for 499,999. A security man discovered a G.I. stuffing a message into bottle number 500,000 ready to throw it overboard. The bottle had been painted red, white and blue and the note gave the name of the ship, the date it sailed and a few other details. It was taken off the G.I. and he was reprimanded.

In December 1941 Churchill visited Washington for talks with General George C. Marshall, US Chief of staff. He asked Churchill how many men should we put on board the ships, knowing each ship's capability was 8,000 but if they were to take no notice of the safety rules they could carry 15,000. Sir Winston replied, "you must judge for yourself the risk you will run". Marshall opted for the maximum number and Churchill said "the troops would have to stand exactly according to instruction without moving". The plan worked and before the summer of 1942 the two Queens had made two more successful trips.

They raced across the North Atlantic despite the presence of the German U-ships and slipped into Firth of Clyde without once so much as a seeing a periscope or a German aircraft, although Hitler had offered $250,000 and an Iron Cross U-boat Commander who sank one of them. It was reported that on 9th November 1942 the U-704, cruising some 200 miles off the west coast of Ireland, fired a salvo

Certificate Number	Transfer No(s).		Date	Number of shares
NILL				NILL

'A' ORDINARY SHARES

SEAWISE & TITANIC
SALVAGE LIMITED

(Incorporated under the Companies Acts 1967 to 1976)

THIS IS TO CERTIFY that

is/are the **Registered Holder**

of *NILL*

'A' ORDINARY SHARES of One Pound each ... to the Memorandum

GIVEN under the Common Seal of the Company on the date written above

Note: No transfer of shares comprised in this Certificate, or any portion thereof will be registered until this Certificate has been surrendered.

Greenaways London

61

of four torpedoes at the QE1 as the liner was traveling towards the United States with a load women and children being evacuated from the British Isles. After two minutes of silent waiting, the Germans felt the underwater shock of an explosion
and raised its periscope to see that the QE1 had slowed to a stop, but then restarted before the submarine could re-load its bowtubes. the German High Command stated that the QE1 has been hit and damaged, but the British Admiralty ignored the claim as there was no proof of there ever being any damage to her.

The invention that made it possible to carry so many was called the standee bunk, a light metal frame of metal tubes supporting six canvas stretchers, to house six sleeping soldiers. They were very strong and light weight and they made it possible to house twice as many troops into the same amount of space.

The last war duties that the Queens performed were to carry the American army home and along with them they took the new brides and new-born American citizens.

Just before war broke out the famous Magna Carta was shipped to America for the 1939 New York World's fair, and afterwards was kept in a vault at the famous Fort Knox in Kentucky for safety. After the war was over the Magna Carta was returned to England on board the QE1 and that was most valuable item that was ever carried by thus ship, apart from all the troops it carried back and forth during the war years.

One by one the ships were refitted and returned to the sea lanes. the QE1 was ready for her first commercial voyage in October 1946. Now in her Cunard colours for the first time, it had taken an army of painters to tackle the task. Her sponsor, Queen Elizabeth, went aboard during her acceptance trials and took her two teenage daughters along for a ride - 20 years on, one of them would give her own name to the QE2.

The QE1 was fully booked. Among the passengers were many of those who had secured their reservations eight years earlier for the ship's original maiden voyage. in 1949 the QE1 tourist berths were sold out for nearly a year ahead, and if a passenger favoured a particular 1st-class cabin a deposit was required six months in advance. All cabins contained the Holy Bible and were also fitted with K.B. radios.

By 1962 Cunard was reporting a loss of £5,000,000 a year. This was due to the fact that jet-liners were freely flying the Atlantic in alittle over seven hours and somewhat cheaper it cost to take a cruise. The QE1 was taken out of service between 1967/69 and was soon to be sold to America, after 27 years of service crossing the Atlantic.

I was probably one of the last people to go on board the QE1 before she was sold. I remember it quite well. It was on a school to Southampton to go and have a last look at the most famous of all the Cunard's liners before she set sail for America to be turned into a floating Hotel. I was about 11 years old at the time but the feeling

I had is one that I will never forget, and the only thing that will better that feeling when we bring the QE1 back to Southampton.

But the salvage of the QE1 will not be easy. It won't be like a normal salvage as she is buried to deep in the sea bed. It will more like an archeological dig with a difference, as it will be a dig under water, and that is the job of the head diver, Steven Bilsby, foster son of Douglas J. Woolley.

In 1972 Doug heard on the radio that the former QE1 had been set alight and sank in Hong Kong harbour. He then found out that it was owned by Hong Kong businessman by the name of Mr C.Y. Tung who had renamed the ship The Seawise University (after himself). Doug found this to be very vain as the QE1 was named after our Queen Mother. The reason behind Mr C.Y. Tung buying the QE1 was the he was pressured into the agreement by the SECRETARY GENERAL OF THE UN, because they needed a floating university for the less well off and it was being fitted out to be turned in to a floating university when it sank.

Doug wrote to Mr Tung and told him of his plan to raise the Titanic and asked if it could be possible to raise The Seawise as a test run for getting his members working together as a team, as they would only have one chance to raise the Titanic . Mr Tung did show interest in Doug's plans and agreed to this.

The Contract

The terms of the contract clearly stated that they - the contractors - would salvage the QE1 and survey and salvage the Titanic for a fee of £40,000, payable on completion of the salvaging of QE1. This would have been possible as there was 40,000 tons of oil on board; also they would have received a further £30,000 from the media coverage. Doug thought that the contract would change his life - and it did - he lost everything, because he put his trust in the hands of those so-called businessmen from Jersey.

After a couple of months Doug decided to go to Hong Kong and see how far they had got the salvaging of QE1. On arrival, he booked himself into the Fougy Hotel in Austin Road, Kowloon. The next morning he went to see the marine department who confirmed that Captain Kingsley had been to see them, but could not report any further. Next he went to visit Mr. C. Y. Tung who said he had nothing to report. With this bout of non-commitment Doug decided that his next stop was the local press, being the Hong Kong Standard and also The Star. The Star gave him front coverage.

Many an iceberg has been identified as the iceberg that sank the Titanic", but this one has a better pedigree than most because a great scar of red paint along the iceberg base. It was photographed near the scene on 15 April.

The Cunard liner Carpathia, which dashed 58 miles through ice-covered waters to rescue the Titanic survivors.

The Titanic's Band.
Leader Wallace Hartley stuck to ragtime while the boats were being lowered

65

Officers of the Leyland liner Californian
She lay within 30 miles of the Titanic all during the sinking

This is a medal which went to every member of the Carpathian crew.
It was presented by Mrs J. J. Brown, the colourful Denver millionairess
who organised the lady oarsmen in Boat 6

SEAWISE & TITANIC SALVAGE LIMITED

P.B. Slade 01-658 0510
C.M. Ramsay 01-251 1826
Telex: 262120

18½ Seckforde Street
London
EC1R 0HN

Your ref:
Our ref: T104/162/54445/C-1.

SEAWISE AND TITANIC SALVAGE LIMITED

Ever since Merritt and Chapman were consulted by the Astor, Widener, and Guggenheim families in 1912, there have been numerous schemes—using everything from Ping-pong balls to helium balloons—to raise the *Titanic*. The most ambitious plan came in 1968 from a firm called *Titanic* Salvage Ltd. The architect of the project was an Englishman, Doug Woolley, who bought up all the salvage claims on the ship and who proposed raising her from her two-mile abyss by means of containers attachable to the hull that would electrolyze seawater into hydrogen. Woolley maintained that "the technical know-how" for raising the *Titanic* existed in fragments all over the world; all that was necessary was for someone to bring the pieces of the technology together "like a jigsaw." Woolley was unable to subscribe the $300 million

Between 1968 and 1978 individuals such as Douglas Woolley, Mark Bamford, Jo and his partner Spencer Sokale spent countless hours planning expeditions to o and retrieve *Titanic*'s remains — and working out how to finance the efforts.

In 1977 a group of West Berlin businessmen set up Titanic-Tresor as a back Douglas Woolley; subsequently they withdrew their support. Also durin_ a company named Seaonics was formed to investigate the wreck's location and for its exploration. This group involved several prominent scientists and explo

In 1979 the British company Seawise & Titanic Salvage was formed. Headed l Ramsay and Philip Slade — with the expertise of Derek Berwin, under-water photo expert and Commander John Grattan, under-water diving consultant — the gr_ funded by industrialist/financier Sir James Goldsmith, who hoped to profit through _ coverage for his magazine, *Now*.

...n the telecast *Return to the Titanic. . . Live*, beamed throughout the United States on __ October 1987, preservationists' concerns were apparently justified. Originating at the Museum of Science and Industry in Paris, the programme purported to display objects recovered from the wreck in a dignified atmosphere and with due respect for survivors' feelings.

Instead, the programme was characterised by loud music, ominous armed guards, and a host (the former star of a police-detective television series) who looked over the artefacts and inquired, 'What is this stuff?'.

On 11 September 1985 a bill was introduced by Walter B. Jones, chairman of the Committee on Merchant Marine and Fisheries, United States House of Representatives, to 'designate the shipwreck of the *Titanic* as a maritime memorial and to provide for reasonable research, exploration and, if appropriate, salvage activities.' The bill was passed by the House on 3 December 1985 and introduced to the Senate on 27 January 1986 by Connecticut's Senator Lowell Weicker, Jr. After committee hearings and minor amendments, the bill was passed on 6 October 1986 and signed into law by President Ronald Reagan on 21 October 1986. Though well-intentioned, the legislation called mainly for an international study of the situation — it had no authority.

Directors: P.B. Slade (Chairman), C.M. Ramsay
Registered in England (No. 1338844) Regd. Office: 18½ Seckforde Street, London EC1R 0HN

___ck.
claim is based on _ities of mercantile _ expert cares fo_ _e. He owns the _d share in the _tar Line, former_ of the stricken was made over to the son of a pas_ among the 1,498 who went down _e Titanic.

been working for _ars to organise the _ge of the Titanic, and _oks as though success _he _____" he said

'It's worth £80m and it's mine'

_tricity is pass_d through _ater, gases are generated. The wreck will be filled with gases produced on the spot from seawater and electricity.

The technique has already been used successfully to raise a heavy coal barge sunk at the mouth of the River Danube.

It could well be that Mr. Woolley does own the Titanic. A spokesman for_ Commercial Union, who_ lost £145,000 when she_ sank, said: "It's quite _ possible. We don't own _ her."

The Cunard Line, who bought the White Star Line, who once owned the Titanic, say they've relinquished all rights.

Douglas Woolley

One man's dream of raising the ship

It's a modern day David and Goliath confrontation. For years Doug Woolley has dreamed and worked towards the realisation of those dreams to raise the ill-fated 46,000 tons RMS Titanic from its watery grave 400 miles off the coast of Newfoundland. He's persevered despite the mocking and the laughter at his plans. Now, few are laughing as a French expedition, backed by millionaires, is in the course of recovering valuables from around the wreck and possibly within it.

'Pirates is what 52 years-old Doug calls them, for he claims legal ownership of the Titanic and its contents. Doug's problem is that, while on paper he appears a millionaire, he is not a rich man, but he is determined he will continue the fight. He knows, however, that money will help him claim items brought up from the wreck as he pursues his plan to raise the ship.

Doug a Gardener Merchant employee, is a kitchen porter at Ford Motor Company, Enfield , and he talked about his plans and aspirations while sitting in his 16th floor flat in a tough part of North London. Apart from Doug and his much loved dog, Flint, his flat is almost a shrine of models, books, legal documents, pictures and correspondence, all relating to the Titanic, as well as prototypes of underwater cameras and diving gear. The story started more than 40 years ago and still continues.

Born in Gambia Terrace, Liverpool (now part of the Anglican Cathedral property), Douglas John Woolley was evacuated from the city when he was three to live with his grandfather in Shrewsbury, from where the family originates.

It was there he heard the story of his grandfather's sisters who planned to go to America on the Titanic's maiden voyage in 1912. At the dockside, despite all her belongings having been loaded, she had a dreadful premonition and refuse to sail. Days later, the 'unsinkable' Titanic hit an iceberg while travelling at 30mph and sank, only a third of the 2,207 people on board surviving.

Little Doug's fascination was further fuelled by a book at his grandfather's which included a story about Captain Smith of the Titanic. Doug began to dream of how it might be possible to raise the ship from the sea-bed.

He returned to Liverpool when he was 12 and while attending Leister Drive Secondary school in Old Swan, carried out experiments with hydrogen gasses to raise weights from underwater . Even the kindest people who were of his hopes, thought it was bizarre.

He left school and had a couple of jobs before returning to Shrewsbury and his grandfather. There for number of years he worked on farms. The raising of the Titanic remained a crucial part of his life.

It still does. Asked why he had never married, he said "It wouldn't be fair. I know it sounds mad to other people, but I have to use all my spare time to realise my ambition."

It was 20 years ago that Doug started a serious assault on the task. By then, he had read everything he could about the ship and disaster. He registered the plan for salvaging the Titanic with Records House and formed the Titanic Salvage Company. He also set about the task of obtaining rights to the ship and contents.

Bringing the Titanic back to Britain

He approached the Board of Trade who told him Cunard were the owners but he would need to search diligently until he found out who all the owners of property were if he were to succeed. That he did. Contract with Cunard White Star resulted in the reaction that it was nothing to do with them. The Titanic was only insured to a quarter of its value (mainly because it was thought to be unsinkable) and eventually Doug traced the underwriters in Sheffield who had the rights. They agreed to waive those rights and to give them to him.

"I think they did that because they did not believe the Titanic could ever be recovered," he said.
He also obtained similar waivers from descendants of those who had property on board.

This activity resulted in some press coverage which in turn brought him a stack of correspondence from people offering help. One letter came from Hungary where a group of scientists had been working in

Budapest on a similar plan for another ship, but which they thought might be of help. They studied Doug's proposals and carried out tests on the Danube over a three year period before reporting back that it was feasible.

Doug's efforts to raise the finance have been less successful. Along with some British businessman, Doug became the principal shareholder in a company called Seawise and Titanic Salvage Ltd., which aimed to raise funds for the project. It all still in being, but the targets were not achieved.

Earlier this year there was renewed hope when an American engineer made contact, then reported he had arranged for a Texas oilman to fund the operation. That too, came to nought and is at the moment subject to legal action by Doug.

There was brighter news and great excitement in April. The auctioneers, Onslows, agreed to stage an auction of items connected with the Titanic at the Park Lane Hotel. More then £100,000 was bid for different items but the biggest single bid was £75,000 for the wheel is only due when the stands has been recovered from the wreck..

So, what of the future? Doug spoke of his current efforts to buy The Shieldhall, a ship at present in Southampton and owned by the southern Water Authority. Isn't he concerned about the French consortium's activities at the wreck?

"We're keeping an eye on what is happening and also trying to make contact with their office. They have only expressed an interest in the property (estimates vary but it is thought by some that the total of £80 million) where as I want to salvage the ship. Even so, I am worried that they are doing could jeopardise my proposals and I shall try to take steps to protect my interest."

What if he is successful, what plans has he for the Titanic? "I would like to see it back in the port of Liverpool, my home town. Just think what a boost to the city's tourist trade that would be!"

Is it feasible ? How can it be done? Certainly Doug Woolley has a plan. An £8 million plan, carefully written and technically checked out. Basically, the scheme is to carry out sufficient repair work on the two sections of the Titanic where they lie. They would then be raised to 200 feet below the surface of the Atlantic and towed to Scotland. That work would take about a year and then there would be a further year's work as she lies in a scottish loch with the whole operation floodlit under water and filmed. At the end of that time it is considered that the two section can be joined and the ship taken down to Liverpool.

Is it more than a dream? Doug has no doubts. "People laughed at me when I first thought of the plan. Now big money people seem to be ignoring my claims. I know that with the right people and appropriate financial backing, we can bring the Titanic back to Britain. I admit that it is a dream but I believe I have proved that it can be a reality."

by MIKE BISSON

A JERSEY COMPANY, Salvors International Ltd., has quoted for the salvage of the liner Queen Elizabeth, which is lying in Hong Kong Harbour after catching fire there and sinking on January 9.

Mr. Brian Hamilton, the managing director of the company, confirmed yesterday that a figure had been quoted for the salvage work, but he did not know if his company would still be prepared to undertake the work.

He explained that since the quote had been put in, a decision had been made to pump out the

oil still held in the tanks of the wreck to avoid any pollution.

There could be as much as 4,000 metric tons of oil there, and there has already been some leakage.

Depending on how long it takes before the owners, insurers and harbour authorities decide that the full salvage work should start, it might be that Salvors would not then be in a position to undertake the job.

Mr. Hamilton explained that the method his company were proposing to use to undertake the salvage might not be acceptable to the owners and harbour authorities—Salvors know of a

new system of salvaging such vessels which could possibly be used.

Although other salvage companies are interested in the salvage and are thought to have made quotes for its salvage, Mr. Stephen Kingsley, Salvors salvage master and a co-founder of the company with Mr. Hamilton and chartered accountant Mr. Michael Forrest, is the only person to have been inside the wreck, which now lies keeled over sticking out of the water.

Mr. Hamilton said that it will have to be moved because it will be a hazard to shipping using a new container berth. It is not known whether the famous 83,700-ton ex-Cunard liner, described by Mr. Hamilton as a "mass of

twisted metal", can be raised and rebuilt, or whether she will have to be cut up for scrap where she lies.

But Mr. Hamilton did say that his salvage master was of the opinion that the vessel could be refloated.

It is still not known what caused the fire on the ship, which was being fitted out as a cruise ship and floating university by Hong Kong shipping magnate Mr. C. Y. Tung at a cost of £44 million.

The results of an enquiry are expected shortly.

Mr. Hamilton said that a full salvage operation could take from 18 months to two years. He was not prepared to disclose what

figure his company had quoted for the work, but he did say that the cost could be in the region of £4m. to £1m. He stressed that with the typhoon season approaching in Hong Kong and the possibility of further damage to the wreck, a figure quoted for the work now would probably not be met by a company after a gap of some months.

Salvors is a new company—it was registered on May 4—and has many other interests apart from the Queen Elizabeth and marine salvage.

Mr. Hamilton said that it could be an important company as far as the Island is concerned, but much would depend on what happens in the next six months.

英文星報專訪
打撈專家妙想天開

伊輪由他接管

給百分二利益予船主

ISLAND NAVIGATION CORPORATION, LTD.

TRIBUNE, MONDAY, NOVEMBER 24, 1969

Briton Places Claim on Wreck of Once Proud Liner Titanic

BY GWEN MORGAN
[Chicago Tribune Press Service]

LONDON, Nov. 23.—"The wreck of it," said Douglas Woolley, his pale blue-gray eyes glowing, "I have lodged my claim, and no one has contested it. My lawyer says I can think of the ship as mine.

"Funny, isn't it, when you own a ship, and it's under water." The ship Woolley says is his is the once proud Titanic. It lies three miles under water.

His claim was filed with the Cunard Steamship company, which owned the Titanic, with the Board of Trade, with the company which insured the liner, and with the receiver of wrecks.

The real miracle is yet to come — if Woolley manages to raise the ship from its ocean grave off Newfoundland, where it sank April 10, 1912, after hitting an iceberg on its maiden voyage.

Woolley is seeking to get the project out of the dream stage, where it has possessed him for half his life. He goes to Budapest, Hungary, today

Woolley believes a lot of young people stand on street corners with nothing to interest them.

He said, "I've always looked for something interesting. Lately a 12-year-old has been going about with me a lot. One day, he'll come up with what's called a fantastic idea. It may not be so fantastic if you examine it with an open mind.

"As for the Titanic," Woolley said, "people still scorn the thought of raising it until it comes off. Then they will say they knew it could be done. I've always believed it's feasible."

He said people thinking about the Titanic today is exactly the way it was when she was launched.

Thinking is Reverse

"She was supposed to be the perfect ship," he said, "But she sank. Now they say you can't get her up. But we can."

Douglas Woolley

Within the last year he has checked with "all possible and previous owners," saying he wanted title in anticipation of salvage.

"They either relinquished title or weren't interested," he said.

Seawise salvage talks

SURVEYING — Woolley will return to England on Thursday to "negotiate from the other end" for a contract for salvaging Seawise University.

Mr Woolley came here earlier this month to talk with the ex-Cunard liner's local agents, Island Navigation Corporation.

"I am flying back to the United Kingdom to complete my negotiations with the head office of Island Navigation and the Protecting and Indemnity Club there."

He has offered to remove the wreck within 18 months. "In return, I shall claim legal title to the hulk," he said.

He hopes to take the wreck to England where it will be preserved for its historical value.

Documents outlining the new offer will be sent to the Marine Department and Island Navigation in Hongkong.

Mr Woolley said a certain amount of profit derived from the wreck would be given to the P and I Club and Island Navigation.

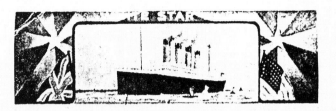

Triple Screw Steamer "TITANIC."

2ND CLASS

APRIL 14, 1912.

DINNER.

CONSOMMÉ TAPIOCA

BAKED HADDOCK, SHARP SAUCE

CURRIED CHICKEN & RICE
SPRING LAMB, MINT SAUCE
ROAST TURKEY, CRANBERRY SAUCE

GREEN PEAS   PURÉE TURNIPS
BOILED RICE
BOILED & ROAST POTATOES

PLUM PUDDING
WINE JELLY   COCOANUT SANDWICH
AMERICAN ICE CREAM
NUTS ASSORTED
FRESH FRUIT
CHEESE   BISCUITS
COFFEE

(Second Class menu for the last dinner.)

Thanks also for the Shropshire cutting - the paper rang me first for a comment on your project. I told them you had done all the right things to establish ownership. I said that the Titanic was a special case in which nothing could be taken for granted but that you had a good chance of success and that the project appeared to be technically feasible.

A W Wakefield

72

R.M.S. "TITANIC"

APRIL 14, 1912.

LUNCHEON.

CONSOMMÉ FERMIER   COCKIE LEEKIE

FILLETS OF BRILL

EGG À L'ARGENTEUIL

CHICKEN À LA MARYLAND

CORNED BEEF, VEGETABLES, DUMPLINGS

FROM THE GRILL.

GRILLED MUTTON CHOPS

MASHED, FRIED & BAKED JACKET POTATOES

CUSTARD PUDDING

APPLE MERINGUE   PASTRY

BUFFET.

SALMON MAYONNAISE   POTTED SHRIMPS

NORWEGIAN ANCHOVIES   SOUSED HERRINGS

PLAIN & SMOKED SARDINES

ROAST BEEF

ROUND OF SPICED BEEF

VEAL & HAM PIE

VIRGINIA & CUMBERLAND HAM

BOLOGNA SAUSAGE   BRAWN

GALANTINE OF CHICKEN

CORNED OX TONGUE

LETTUCE   BEETROOT   TOMATOES

CHEESE.

CHESHIRE, STILTON, GORGONZOLA, EDAM,
CAMEMBERT, ROQUEFORT, ST. IVEL,
CHEDDAR

Iced draught Munich Lager Beer 3d. & 6d. a Tankard.

(First Class menu for lunch the last day afloat - this was
the meal Bruce Ismay ate with Captain Smith.)

(Payoff slip - note that the men's pay stopped as the waters closed over the Titanic's rudder.)

The Titanic on the ways at Harland & Wolff

The Olympic and Titanic at Belfast. Probably the
only picture of the two sisters together

(Loading luggage onto the *Titanic* shortly before sailing time.)

Extract from Doug's Press Diary:

The *Queen* can float again

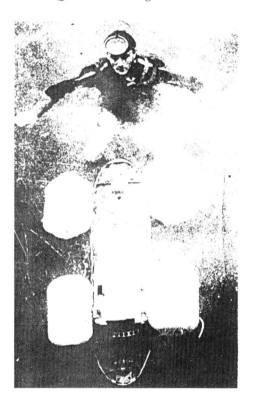

(The salvage method)

(RMS Queen Elizabeth)

A British salvage expert is confident that the Queen Elizabeth can float again - but says she will not be able to sail. Mr Douglas J. Woolley (37) who made headlines with his plans to salvage the Titanic is in Hong Kong to meet officials of the island Navigation Company. "Queen Elizabeth can be salvaged and float again," he said. It can be preserved but it will not be able to sail again under its own steam. Mr Woolley estimates the cost of refloating the Queen as not over $7 million. "Personally, I would like to see the Queen turned into a museum," he said. Then the paper goes on to say how he will use compressed air to raise the Queen.

QE1 in Hong Kong harbour after being damaged by fire

Doug's next step was TV/radio - this was to get himself established in Hong Kong. He then had further meetings at the office of Mr C. Y. Tung, with the sub manager of his company Mr M. H. Liang. Doug asked him, during a meeting, who did the Seawise belong to and his reply was "we at this time do not know and are not certain".

So because of his involvement with the contract, he now classed QE1 as an open vessel. This enabled him to make a claim of salvage on her which he did in the correct and proper manner and this was then reported in Hong Kong Standard. As a result of this the Standard took him out to look at the Queen.

Mr Douglas Woolley, who is planning to raise the Titanic, says he now has seven or eight sources prepared to put up the £30,000 to £40,000 needed to start the salvage operation and is investigating which offer would give the best return. (The link company is Salvors of Jersey, C.I.)

This latest offer is from POOM International, of Hong Kong, from where Mr Woolley, of Baldock, recently had a request from a 16-year-old boy to join the salvage operation. This was not possible - instead he has become an honourary uncle to the boy, Adam Tang.

The raising of the Titanic - Plan given go-ahead by Sheffield businessman's action

Plans for raising from the ocean bed the famous liner Titanic, which sank off Newfoundland on its maiden voyage in April 1912, have now been given the final go-ahead, following the action of a Sheffield businessman.

He is Mr W. Gordon Laycock, of Sand Rock, Garden House, Tickhill, near Doncaster, whose grand father is thought to have been involved with liner when she was built.

"When the Titanic was lost my grandfather suffered considerable financial losses and we think he was a sub-contractor or perhaps an underwriter for the ship," said Mr Laycock.

"His firm, W. S. Laycock Ltd, (now Laycock Engineering Co, of Millhouses, Sheffield), used to make equipment for steamships and railways."

But after consultations with other members of the family, Mr Gordon Laycock has now signed over any compensation rights they might have to the group planning to raise the ship, so that they can get on with the job.

This ship - one of the biggest liners ever built - was almost half a mile long and had a displacement of 46,000 tons. When it sank after striking an iceberg at speed, 1,513 of 2,224 people on board died.

The recovery operation is being launched by an international group including scientists and other experts from the United States, Hungary, Sweden and Britain, but with the great ship lying at a depth of three miles it will be no easy operation.

If successful the ship will be taken to New York to be cleaned and made ready for the trip back to Southampton, said Mr Douglas Woolley, chairman of the Titanic Salvage Company, who hopes it will be put on show as other great ships have been.

Malagasy jail pair "in good spirits"

British Consulate officials have now been allowed to see the former Hayling man held in jail in Malagassy - formerly Madagascar - since September.

Mr Stephen Kingsley (39), whose home is at Longfield, Kent, was working on the Indian Ocean island on marine salvage operation with a colleague,

Mr Christopher Williams (35) of Chislehurst.

Both men were arrested on charges of endangering the security of the state and have also been charged with having no work or residents' permit and of unlawfully using telecommunications equipment on board ship. Foreign Office officials have not been allowed to contact the men since their arrest.

A Foreign Office spokesman explained: "The British Honourary Consul and a Counsellor from the High Commission in Dar-Es-Salaam were allowed to see the two men on 8 December.

We understand Mr Kingsley went into hospital on 24th November with dysentery. We do not know whether he has been discharged, but he came to the prison to see our representative in December and he is said to be in the hands of a good doctor."

The men told officials they had unimpaired access to legal advisers of their own choice and that they were both in good spirits.

"Mr Kingsley and Mr Williams face political and civil charges, but we are hoping the political charges will be dropped.

"We understand the case is proceeding in the usual way and the nearest British Consul is keeping a check on the situation."

Mr Kingsley's mother-in-law, Mrs D. Lawrence, lives at North Crescent,

Hayling. Mrs Pat Kingsley, his wife, commented: "The Foreign Office has been in touch with me, but I am still very uncertain about what is happening."

Mr Kingsley and Mr Williams were aboard the Panamanian registered Orient London, when the vessel was stopped and the authorities claimed its papers were not in order.

The men helped to salvage the ship, which had developed leaks in the hold and was being towed towards Malagasy.

Formed Titanic Salvage Company

Mr Woolley, Once completely alone in this project and considered something of a crackpot, is not alone in his project now. Indeed, he has drawn around him a twenty-five-strong team, which goes to make up the 'Titanic Salvage Company', a strongly international team of which he is chairman.

The publicity for this scheme started on a very small scale, with an article in a local paper. It has since found its way to the most improbable corners of the earth.

Two scientists in Budapest read the story and thought this was just the way to prove their new salvage method works. In America it reached the ears of Hugh Carlon of Bel Air, Maryland, who liked the idea and wanted to join in - and so the scheme has snowballed.

The method Mr Woolley plans to use to raise the liner is basically fairly simple. Perfected by two Hungarian scientists it is based on general assumption that hydrogen is lighter than air.

It is estimated that it will take seven days for the ship to be lifted from bottom to top. The method has been checked and re-checked for flaws, and Mr Woolley is sure it can be done.

They did tests in 1971. Doug's tests were in 1950, 51, 52 and 1996. Tests will now be made by Clive Mead and R.J. Amphett.

Hong Kong Standard
Police probe QE blaze

A top detective is to investigate the fire which destroyed the Queen Elizabeth liner, it was revealed in the Hong Kong press.

The police were called in by official Marine Department investigator Mr N.J. Mathew.

A police spokesman confirmed that the detective has been assigned to work with Mr Mathew, but declined to comment further.

Mr Mathew was appointed by the Director of Marine on Monday to conduct a preliminary inquirey into the fire.

He will be writing a report which will eventually go to Governor, Sir Murray MacLehose. The report is expected to be completed within a month.

Earlier yesterday, there was mounting speculation that the police would be called in to investigate a right-wing newspaper report that left-wing unionists working on board the ship may have deliberately set the liner ablaze.

Two huge Chinese characters each albeit eight feet long and reading "China" and "America" were also reported to have been found scribbled on deck of the wreck near one of the funnels.

The writing had escaped the inferno that raged through the ship on Sunday and Monday.

The newspaper report also said that the plum blossom decorations could have "sparked off the sabotage" as this is the emblem of the Nationalist Chinese party, the Kuomintang.'

This was discussed at the meeting in London on 14th May 1972 with Kingsley, Hamilton, Slade and Mr D.J. Woolley at the meeting of Salvors Ltd and Seawise Salvage Co.

London Daily News

The Titanic, the passenger liner which sank after hitting an iceberg on its maiden voyage in 1912, is believed to lie off the coast of Newfoundland.

Mr Woolley and his team have narrowed the position down to within a 30-mile radius, and if they are successful in raising the £8 million needed for such a project, things could start to move next year.

They plan to raise the enormous ship using balloons - a system which makes it, without a doubt, the most ambitious salvage operation of all time.

Titanic task for camera

The test on underwater camera equipment-which could be used in the rasing of the Titanic - will go ahead at Milton Keynes' Blue Lagoon.

The date has been provisionally set for Saturday, 20th July. But much depends on wether an experimental camera can be built on time, and how crowded the lake is on that day.

If the experiment is successful, the camera-designed by Douglas Woolley, organiser of the daring salvage project - will be tested again in operation to raise the Queen Elizabeth liner from the bottom of Hong Kong harbour.

Nicknamed 'The Dart' because of its long, cylindrical shape, the camera will be weighted to take it directly to the lake bottom.

A trigger mechanism will then release the main body containing electrical components - and a substance lighter than air to cause the camera to turn over on itself and take a photograph as it rises gently to the surface.

The Dart's design has been modified by a new recruit to the Titanic project, Phil Smith. Phil, 31, of Beadlemead, Netherfield was introduced to Mr Woolley through project diver Steven Bilsby - and was immediately fuelled by his Titanic dream.

"It was his enthusiasm really," he said. "It is something new and different. Alot of people have tried and got nowhere, but I think we can do it."

DOUGLAS JOHN FAULKNER
WOOLLEY

CAPTAIN SMITH'S CAREER

FROM THE RAMMED OLYMPIC
TO THE ILL-FATED TITANIC

AN UNLUCKY RECORD

By a remarkable coincidence Captain E.J Smith R.N.R.,who was in command of the Titanic, was captain of the Olympic when, last September, she was in collision with the cruiser Hawke off Cowes.

As the vessel was subject to compulsory pilotage, the responsibility for her course was not Commander Smith's but that of the Trinity pilot who was in charge.

Captain Smith entered the White Star service thirty-eight years ago, and has commanded in turn many of the White Star cracks, including the Old Republic, the Britannic, and the Germanic, and for nine years was in command of the Majestic.

During South African War he twice carried troops out in the Majestic, bringing back sick and wounded on the return trips. He was decorated by the King for his services.

He next commanded the Baltic, and then the Adriatic. Then, on the sailing of the Olympic, he was transferred to her, and finally to the Titanic.

He held an extra master's certificate, and was an honourary commander of the royal Naval Reserve.

Other leading officers were Surgeon W.F.N. O'Loughlin, Assistant-Surgeon J.E. Simpson, Purser H.W. McElroy and R.L. Barker,and Chief Steward A. Latimer.

BRAVE MAN'S FIRST ORDER:
"CLOSE THE EMERGENCY DOOR"

Mr Geore A. Barden states: "I saw Captain Smith while I was in the water. He was standing on the deck all alone.

"Once he was swept down by wave, but managed to get to his feet again.

"Then as the boat sank, he was again knocked down by a wave, and then disappeared from view. " - Reuter.

Robert Hichens, the Titanic's quatermaster, says Captain Simth's first words after the collision were: "Close the emergency doors".

"They're already closed, sir," replied Mr Murdock, the first officer.

"Send for the carpenter, and tell him to sound the ship," said the captain, but the carpenter never came, for he had been killed in the first crash.

"I was at the wheel," continued the quatermaster, "until 12.25, when Second officer Lightoller told me to take charge of a lifeboat and load it with ladies. I did so."

Captain Smith's self-sacrifice and heroism, even after the bridge had disappeared beneath the waves, has been commended by all.

Before he was literally washed from his post of duty he called through his megaphone, "Be British!" to the mass below. Later he was seen in the act of helping those struggling in the water, refusing an opportunity to save himself.

Capatin Smith

Captain Smith was the Captain of the Titanic on her maiden voyage. He was born in Staffordshire and grew up to become a very proud, man proud to be British and proud of his job, as he was Commander of the White Star Fleet and Captain of the Olympic which is a sister ship to the Titanic. She was in service until 1935 when she was retired and scrapped after 24 years service. While he was in command of the Olympic she collided with another vessel, for what reasons we do not know, still Captain Smith was given the command of the Titanic on that maiden voyage.

The story tells that after the Titanic hit the iceberg Captain Smith gave the order to man the lifeboats and then he went up to the bridge and armed himself with a pistol in order to shoot himself. But this was not true. He went to the bridge to get a flare gun so as to shoot a distress signal into the air, in the hope any nearby vessels would come to his aid. After he had fired the gun, he was seen to jump into the sea and swim to a small child. He grabbed her and swam her to a near by lifeboat and put the child in it.

It was said that Captain Smith was never seen again, but about a year later, a tramp appeared on the streets of New York who claimed that he was Captain Smith. Some people must have believed him because when he died they mummified his body and it is kept somewhere in New York.

FACTS ABOUT THE TITANIC

The Titanic was impressive enough without embellishment.

Her weight 46,328 gross tons - 66,000 tons displacement.

Her dimensions: 882.5 feet long, 92.5 feet wide, 60.5 feet from waterline to boat deck, or 175 feet from keel to the top of her four huge funnels. She was, in short 11 stories high and four city blocks long.

The Titanic had two sets of four-cylinder reciprocating engines, each driving a wing propeller and a turbine driving the centre propeller. This combination gave her 50,000 registered horsepower but she could easily develop at least 55,000 horsepower.

At full speed she could make 24-25 knots.

Perhaps her most arresting feature was her WATERTIGHT construction. She had a double bottom and was divided into 16 watertight compartments. These were formed by 15 watertight bulkheads running clear across the ship.

Nevertheless, she could float with any two compartments flooded, and since no one could imagine anything worse than a collision at the juncture of two compartments, she was labelled unsinkable.
See: Lady Hobatay.
The (unsinkable) Titanic was launched at Belfast shipyards of Harland and Wolff on 31st May 1911.

The last recorded position of the Titanic was 41° 46`N 50° 14`W. It was believed that there were three ships in the area at the time, the nearest being a Norveginan fishing boat, M.V. Samson, which did not answer the Titanic's SOS as it was fishing illegally and did not want to face any legal battles. the next nearest was the M.V. Antinovs, a British freighter from Hull - the last date this vessel was in a British port was 16th November 1911 in Hull. The California was the third nearest to the Titanic, at about 25-30 miles north of the accident,but none of these three ships responded as they thought that the flares were fireworks and that they were having some kind celebration or party. The S.S. Carpathia was a bit further away, as soon as Captain Rostron heard the Titanic's distress call, he gave the order to his crew to race to the scene to aid the ship, but when he got there all they could find was the Titanic's lifeboats and about 705 of her passengers and crew - but this was not until the following morning.

Titanic going down

Captain Smith (right) with Purser McElroy taken when the Titanic stopped at Queenstown on 11 April.

Chief officer Henry T. Wilde was ordered by Captain Smith at 12.05 am to uncover the lifeboats.

WRECKS LAWS

(extracts) (comments in brackets
by Doug Woolley)
1. There are two Acts which deal with
wreck.

a. The Merchant Shipping at 1894
(part IX), covering wreck, salvage and the
Receiver of Wreck system.

b. The Protection of Wrecks Act 1973,
covering the protection of important or
dangerous wrecks and wrecks sites.

2. The expression 'wreck' means loosely
the remains of a ship, her cargo, tackle,
furniture armament and the personal possessions of those who travelled in her. It
may also cover anything thrown or washed
overboard as well as abandoned property,
i.e. property which the insurers or owners
say they have 'abandoned' rather that
'have no interest in'. (Cunard have no
claims.)

3. The objects of The Receiver of Wreck
system are to:

a. Stop items of wreck being appropriated
by people to whom it does not belong;
(such at the US and French Salvors)

b. Find the owners of recovered items of
wreck, if possible, and return their property to them;

c. ensure that law abiding finders of such
property receive an appropriate payment,
or keep items of wreck, whether owners
are found or not. (All legal steps have
been kept to the letter on the QE1 & the
Titanic.)

4. Finding an object does not make it the
property of the finder, even if it is found
outside British waters (more that 12 miles
from the coastline).

5. The rights to items of the wreck lie
firstly with the owner. (These rights have
been handed to D.J. Woolley.)

6. The Receiver of Wreck does not get
involved with disputes between Salvors.
It must go to court.

7. Salvors should not assume a wreck has
no owner. (Corrected this as being met to
the full and notice placed in this press.)

8. Not every finder (Grimm, Ballard and
later finders) necessarily has salvage
rights. Nor does the raising of the items
confer any rights to a site. (D.J.W. made
his claims on the Titanic and the QE1 in
accordance to the law. The US courts
have no bearing in these matters and the
claims of the Americans are not valid.)

9. Historic wrecks

a. Can be designated under the 1973 Act
to protect the wreck. (NB: for the next
two years only, Hong Kong are still
classed as British waters.)

b. Anyone who interferes with a designated site without a license is guilty of an
offence. (This is a British law, but did the
last American to find the Titanic, who
stole, everything he could lay his hands on
for commercial purposes, have any permission to do so? Ballard was more care-
ful and made it clear his activities were of
an archeological rather than a commercial
nature.)

c. Recoveries from historic wrecks will not normally be allowed unless conservation facilities (i.e. a museum) are known in advance.

10. All parts of this are subject to the salvage contract made by Salvors and Offshore Management Ltd and those founders and Directors, and are a subject of the Royal Court of Jersey, C.I. and the Supreme Court of Hong Kong.

11. Notice of the legal claims were proclaimed in the City Recorder, London and with other Press outlets at the time that caused a lot of consternation in London on 27th February 5th March 1981. This notice was to comply with Merchant Shipping Acts of 1894 and the contract made in Jersey, C.I. in 1972 on both the QE1 and the RMS Titanic.)

These Wreck Laws were explained to one of the members of the team and he was seen to sign his signature of approval. That member was Leigh Huggins.

Flint bathing in the dock of the QE1's bay

Hong Kong News on Salvage plans of QE1 and D.J. Faulkner Woolley 1972.

Douglas John Faulkner-Woolley -1948-

Flint resting after a busy day

Flora Kean flicking through Titanic memoirs

Commander Grattan R.N Story

On the strength of his discoveries he says: "A lot of accepted beliefs about the Titanic are nothing more than myth."

He dismisses explosions or being ripped apart by the speed of her descent through the Atlantic. He believes she is in one piece and probably the right way up, in 12,000 ft of water.

Commander Grattan claims to know the exact position of the Titanic.

By going back to the information collected soon after the disaster and by checking bits of evidence against each other, he has produced a "search area" a short distance from the official position of the wreck, which is 41 degrees 46 minutes north, 50 degrees 14 minutes west.

Then, he says. he obtained "a certain piece of information" which proved that a large hull is present in that area. He gives no more details about this "piece of information" but it is possible that he has been given advice by military sources.

It is known that major powers have anti-submarine equipment capable of producing detailed maps of the sea bed. But locating the wreck is less than half the battle. The big hazard in all the schemes to make contact with the Titanic in the immense pressure that exists at 12,000 ft below the surface of the sea.

The only manned vessels capable of operating at the depth are used exclusively by the military. So Commander Grattan's team is planning to use unmanned, remote controlled submarines to photograph the vessel, inside and out.

(This was before Mr Grimm and Mr Ballard)

The Ray Seager Story

The dream of seeing the Titanic in dry dock returned to her former glory is so intense for a West Kingsdown man he intends to raise £150 million to make it a reality.

Mr Ray Seager of Multon Road, has enlisted a salvage company to make an initial feasibility study and plans to finance the venture by selling shares in a new company.

"The earning potential of the boat is massive," he said. "So I will raise the finance on long term credit."

Mr Seager, aged 38 became interested in the Titanic during the 1960s after reading the book "Raise the Titanic" by Clive Cusler.

Since then his interest has escalated and he has joined societies, visited auctions and ploughed a few thousand pounds into his hobby.

A year ago he met a man with similar desire to see the Titanic raised, and plans have been becoming more concrete ever since.

He is sympathetic to those who wish for the boat to be left as a grave for those who died but said that he had received a letter from a woman whose father owned a haberdashery shop on the boat and died in the disaster encouraging him in his efforts.

"Any one interested will be able to come at any time during the cleaning of the boat to see that we will treat her with reverence and that we are not merely following a money spinner," he said.

The boat will be lifted by placing cradles underneath and then towed under water to docks in Liverpool or Scotland.

Mr Seager, a lorry driver, who is a mortgage broker in his spare time, has a wife and two children. He is used to people being fairly sceptical about his ideas and his wife is now becoming increasingly supportive as plans look more concrete.

"This is a serious venture," he said. "Most people have a dream of winning the pools. My dream is to see people looking round that boat and I will stand by with my hands in my pockets saying 'I have done it, I have brought her up'."

Lifting the S.S. Titanic
by Des Raive

Lifting ships since time immemorial, has been a lucrative industry, albeit fraught with danger. One of the biggest prizes still left on the bottom of the sea is mighty passenger liner "Titanic". She came to grief after hitting the cutting edge of an iceberg, which produced a 300 foot long slit, so long that the water-tight bulkhead could not manage to keep the vessel afloat. In two hours and twenty minutes she sank, with a great loss of life. Many passengers and crew however were

rescued the following day by the Cunarder S.S. Carpthia.

A Liverpool born, west country educated man D.J. Woolley, now living in Ilford has, for the last 15 years, been developing the idea of lifting this ship from the seabed. She is about two and a half miles down, only thirty nine miles from the Grand Banks, roughly 430 miles South East of Cape Race. It is known to within 18 miles where she is to be found, and echo-sounding experts are quite confident it would be a simple matter to locate her. The method is towing what is known as a "deep sea fish" so that the sonar waves have not as far to travel as from a surface operating echo-sounder. (This was done in 1953 with the ship M.V. Help from Southampton.)

Mr Woolley has made very intensive research on the subject to the wreckage of this famous White Star Liner and also the QE1 in Hong kong. He would use 200 pontoons with electric current which would produce enough hydrogen to lift the ship. The only thing which cannot be decided yet is how to get these "floating gasworks" to lift the ship, because the attachment of the pontoons will depend upon the position of the hulk, to be ascertained by close-circuit television cameras carrying, of course, the necessary light in the dark deep. (This will be done by Salvors Ltd of Jersey, C.I. and offshore Management Ltd of same and their founders.)

It is estimated that the total value of the ship including a vast quantity of gold bullion and jewellery, should be about

£80,000,000. Nobody else has staked a claim. The underwriters have paid out the loss two generations ago, and have officially stated that there is now no claim at all. So Mr Woolley has made officially, and nobody is disputing it. He has to find the necessary backing. It is refreshing to find somebody who is trying to solve problems by new thinking, even if it is to be a Titanic lifting operation!

Mr Woolley thought the QE1 would provide a good opportunity to test his salvage method, even though the conditions were quite different. Where as the Titanic was lying under about 2.5 miles of water, most of the QE1 was still visible above the surface. As it turned out, the Titanic salvage method was too dangerous for the QE1 as the wrecked liner was lying near oil containers and buildings. Using the electrolysis process there is always the ever-present danger of an explosion from the gas. Mr woolley decided however, to make a bid for the salvage of the QE1. He thought that if he could pull it off he would be sure to get the financial support he needed for the Titanic's salvage.

Contact was made between Woolley's company and a Channel Island-based salvage company, Salvors Ltd of St Helier, Jersey, and a salvage expert, Captain Stephen Kingsley, went to Hong Kong and carried out a full survey of the QE1. On the basis of his report, Woolley's company submitted a tender for the salvage of the ship to the Protection and Indemnity Club of London, acting on behalf of the vessel's owner, Mr C.Y Tung.

Flora Kean

Paddington's link to the Titanic, Flora Kean, is backing a plan to raise the sunken vessel and turn it into a permanent museum.

Miss Kean, of Sussex Gardens, was a baby when her father died on the ship where he worked as a hairdresser.

He had his own salon and jewellery boutique on board and Miss Kean would like to see the jewellery on public display along with all the other valuables locked in the sunken tomb.

Mr Woolley is heading a plan to raise it to the surface and have it docked in Southampton as a permanent museum.

Miss Kean, 76, thinks it is an ambitious plan because it will cost about £18 million.

She said: "I'm excited about it. It would be wonderful to raise it if it was possible, but there is always a big but". "I would like Mr Woolleys dream to come true," she said.

Miss Kean's plans for the ship go one step further. She would like to see all profits from the museum going to charity. This is hardly surprising because this energetic woman is an active member of the Women's Royal Voluntary Service. Every day she is busy organising the meals-on-wheels service in Kensington and Chelsea.

She said: "We need so much money for charity, I would like it to help people in need.
(End of press cuttings)

Flora is now 84 years old and is still working. She works voluntarily at Wormwood Scrubs Prison looking after the dinners for the inmates.

Copy of a letter sent to Doug from Flora:

Dear Douglas

This letter will tell you that I cede to you my goods that should be intact in the Titanic, on the understanding that they cannot be sold or disposed of at any time and must remain with the Titanic for all time,.

Sincerely
Flora (kean)

Extracts from the Minutes of Meetings:

Meeting held at the Avon Court Hotel on Sunday 14th May 1972

The meeting was called at the request of Salvors Ltd, to discuss proposals to be made by them, affecting the contract between themselves and Mr Woolley (for Titanic and Seawise Salvage Co).

The meeting was opened by Mr Brian Hamilton of Salvors who was also elected Chairman.

Those present:
Mr Brian Hamilton
Mr Stephen Kingsley (Captain)
Mr Peter Bajic
Mr Rister Kosjovic
Miss M. Ward

Titanic & Seawise Salvage:
Mr Douglas J. Woolley
Mr Philip Slade
Mr John Dade
Mr John Gilbert
Mr M. Steven Noades
Mr Philip Brown
Mr Iain Gurr

1. Messrs Hamilton and Kingsley were voted on to the board of 'Titanic & Seawise' by a unanimous vote.

2. The agreements signed by Salvors and Mr Woolley were shown to the meeting, and it was stated by Mr Hamilton, that the retainer fees mentioned in the agreements, would become payable on completion of the Contracts. Mr Kingsley added that since the Queen Elizabeth (Seawise) contained 40,000 tons of fuel oil, this could be pumped off, and disposed of at £1 per ton, resulting in an income of £40,000, out of the retainer on that job, thereby releasing in the income from hull of any lien, and making it gross profit.

3. Mr Kingsley said that he had surveyed the ship in Hong Kong, and had obtained plans from the sub Manager of Sea Island Navigation. (These plans we understood later, should have been returned to Sea Island, but never were.) He gave a brief outline of the job at hand and how the salvage could be achieved.

Meeting of the directors of Seawise & Titanic Salvage Limited held at 45 Beech Street, London EC1 on 25th November 1977

Present:
  P.B.J Slade (Chairman)
  R.J. Wilkins
  C.M. Ramsay

In attendance: D.J. Woolley

Minutes of a meeting held on 17th November were presented and approved.

Mr Blundell, Mr Slade confirmed that a telex message had been sent explaining the delay in the formation of the company. It was agreed that he represented the company's most promising source of finance. it was resolved that Mr Blundell be offered a directorship.

Explanatory memorandum: it was agreed that the memorandum should be spirally bound. An outline should be ready by 30th November. Mr Wilkins presented his notes covering the survey and equipment to be used.

Letter heading: A design for the company letter heading was presented by Mr Slade and approved.

Public relations: Agreed that Mr D. Berwin should be appointed public relations officer. He would be offered a retention fee plus a percentage of receipts from sales of stories, photographs etc.

Allotment of shares
D.J Woolley was allotted 55 (fifty-five) shares

P.B.J Slade	15 (fifteen)
R.J. Wilkins	15 (fifteen)
C.M. Ramsay	15 (fifteen)
	100

Filing of forms: Resolved that from PUC2 be filed to record the above.

The meeting was then closed.

Meeting of directors of Seawise & Titanic Salvage Limited held at 45 Beech Street, London EC1 on 11th April 1978

Present:
  P.B.J. Slade (Chairman)
  C.M. Ramsay
  J. Wilkins

In attendance: D.J. Woolley

Capital change: It was resolved that the 100 ordinary shares of £1 be sub-divided into 500 ordinary shares of 20p.

Share transfers: Philip Slade requested that one third of his holdings of 75 20p shares be transferred to his wife. This was approved.

Aquatech: Mr Slade's meeting with the directors of Aquatech was discussed. Mr Slade said that Aquatech would be willing to receive fully paid shares in the Company as payment for their services. This arrangement was approved and it was agreed that a contract should be drawn up.

Titanic public relations: The contract between the Company and T.P.R. was discussed, particularly arrangements for the payment of the 20% fee.

Kelvin Hughes: Talks with Kelvin Hughes have resulted in their oral agreement to provide equipment suitable for locating the Titanic at a normal fee of £55 per day. In return Kelvin Hughes would receive as much publicity as Titanic Public Relations can negotiate.

Vessel: Mr Slade read out details of vessel that may be available for search. As Kelvin Hughes have indicated that a larger vessel that originally costed for will be required, it was agreed that Mr Slade should continue with his enquiries.

Mr Blundell: The delay is sending detailed costs of final survey to Mr Blundell was pointed out by Mr Slade and he emphasised the urgency of this matter. It was agreed that schedules should be sent, together with apologies as soon as possible.

The meeting was then closed.

Meeting of the Directors of Seawise & Titanic Salvage Limited held at 45 Beech street, London EC1 on Monday 13th August 1979

Present:
 P.B. Slade
 C.M. Ramsay

I.S.E. a telex message recently received from Mr James McFarlane of I.S.E. giving accurate costing for the project was discussed. It was agreed that a copy would be shown to John Grattan.

Mirror Books: An offer from Mirror Books to buy UK publishing rights of possibly three books covering the operation was discussed. It was agreed that we should attempt to find out weather the offer is a reasonable one. Other publishers may have approached and if this is done all care should be taken to ensure confidentiality is maintained. It was agreed that George Greenfield should be approached

Sponsorship: In view of the tight time scale on which we will be operating it was agreed that approaches should now be made to prospective sponsors. Initially this should be via close introductions in order to ensure that Cavenham's story is protected.

Registrar of Companies: A letter recently received from the Registrar of companies, informing us that they had a complaint that the company had not held an AGM was discussed. It was agreed that copies of minutes of the AGM, notice calling the meeting, attendance list etc should be sent in reply.

Who owns the Seawise?

A businessman from Liverpool yesterday claimed he would "nail a notice on a mast" to claim his right to salvage the half-submerged hulk of the Seawise University.

The businessman, Mr Douglas Woolley, has been in Hongkong for more than a month in an attempt to get a salvage contract.

He claimed that during a recent meeting Mr M. H. Liang, sub-manager of Island Navigation Corporation, told him: "We, at this time, are uncertain as to who the owners of the hulk) are."

Mr Woolley said he now considered the hulk to be an "open" one.

"I am invoking a law whereby, if a ship is declared a total wreck, which the Seawise is, the person who puts a legal claim for the salvaging is entitled to carry it through."

R.C. Amphlett

Steven Bilsby

Captain Smith

Meeting of the Directors of Seawise & Titanic Salvage Limited held at 45 Montagu Square, London W1 at 6.30 pm on Thursday 6th September 1979

Cavenham communications: Mr Slade relayed to Mr Ramsay the problem that had arisen over Cavenham's insistence that John Grattan reveals the exact location of the Titanic to "Now" magazine. After considerable difficulty Mr Grattan had been persuaded to reveal the position in a letter to be handed to Cavenham's solicitors on the understanding that the position would not be revealed to any other party. A meeting had arranged to hand over the letter to Cavenham's solicitors in Saddler's Hall, Gutter Lane. Mr Ramsay agreed to attend as the Seawise representative.

I.S.E: As Mr Slade could not accept the in action to a reception held at the Canadian High Commission given by I.S.E. it was agreed that Mr Ramsay would attend and could then inform I.S.E. that they had been chosen to conduct the survey.

Sponsorship: Mr Slade informed Mr Ramsay of the approaches he made to various companies seeking sponsorship and gave details of the companies.

Meeting of the Directors of Seawise & Titanic Salvage Limited held at 18 Sekforde Street, London EC1 on 13 August 1982

Investments: It was agreed to take a further partial profit on the holding in O.R.E. by the sale of the 160 shares and re-invest the proceeds in 1,000 London Private Health Group.

Shareholders: Further to the point raised at the directors meeting held in March it was agreed that if possible an offer of stock not held by the directors would be made at the same time the Report and Accounts for year ended April 1982 were circulated.

Lonrho: The purchase of 450 shares in Lonrho, previously agreed on the telephone by the directors, was ratified.

Titanic Memorial, Southampton

Ricky

An early day example of a superimposed photograph showing someone who wasn't really there.

Titanic's vast proportions

The Jersey office of Salvors Limited in 1972.

|| || ক্যামেরায় ফজলুল হকের নিজের হাতে তোলা নিজের ছবি ||

ঢাকার আশরায়াবাদ বললে, হয়তো অনেকেই চিনবেন না। তবে কামরাংগীর চর বললে, অনেকেই চিনতে পারবেন। সেই কামরাংগীর চরের ছেলে ফজলুল হক। পড়ত, ওয়েস্ট ব্লেন্ড হাই স্কুলে। তারপর, একদিন বাবার সাথে যোগ দিল, সাত সমুদ্র তের নদীর পারে বিলেতে চলে যাসার জন্যে। কুস্টের না হলেও সংগ্রামী সংসার। তাই ফজলুল হককে বাবার কস্ট লাঘব করার জন্যে যোগ দিতে হল কাজে।

তারপর? কাজে যোগ দেয়ার পরে আর কিইবা বাকী থাকে? সংসার সমরাংগনে যুদ্ধ করে যেতে হয়। বড় হবার সুর হয়তো আর জানালা দিয়ে আসে না।

কিন্তু ফজলুল হকের বেলায় তা পুরোপুরি হল না। কাজ করলেও, তার চোখ কান খোলা। দুনিয়াটায় কোথায় কি হচ্ছে সেদিকে তার নজর।

ফজলুল হক যেখানে কাজ করত সেখা-

ন্নে কেউ কি কখনো টাইটানিক ওঠাবার কথা ভাবে?

কিন্তু ফজলু ভালোভাবেই চেনে উলী সাহেব কে। আর যাইহোক, উলী সাহেব মাথা খারাপ নয়। এর মধ্যে নিশ্চয়ই একটা বিরাট কিছু না হলেও, অন্য কিছু রহস্য আছে।

তাই একদিন ফজলু ধরে ফেলল, মিঃ ডগলাস উলীকে। কি ব্যাপার ভাই? আপনি করতেটা কি চাচ্ছেন?

উলী সাহেব ফজলুর আগ্রহ দেখে প্রীত বোধ করলেন। তখন তাকে তার মনের কথা খুলে ও বুঝিয়ে বললেন।

বললেন, আজ থেকে অনেক বছর আগের কথা। তোমার তো বটেই, আমারও জন্মের আগের কথা। বিলেতে একটা বিরাট ও চমৎকার জাহাজ তৈরী করা হয়। এটা লম্বায় ছিল ১০০ ফুট। ওজনে ছিল ৬৬ হাজার টন। বৃটিশ ইঞ্জিনিয়র আর

SMILLER
A Member of Doug's team very loyal.
BENGAL NEWS

96

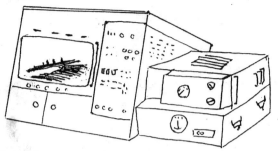

| 0 - 500 m |
| ECHOSOUNDER |
| VTR |

Until the late fifties commercial interest in deep
diving was restricted to the occasional salvage
operation with proffessional divers rarely operating
below 200ft. But onee gas had been struck in the north
sea in 1965 men emerged who could dive sufficiently
deepto build and later service the new oilfield
developments.
Breathing a mixture of helium ando oxygen they
were helping to create an industry outo of saturation diving.

Filming will also help the divers and people working
on the surface",
"Ironically, we can see more on the television monitors
on board than the divers sometimes can"

That point of the Operation is where Woolley hopes to
receive what he intends tobe the first instalment on
the Titanic project. For a national newspaper has already
offered him £50,000 for a photograph of the wreckage which
is recognisable as having come from the ship, using our
sonar method , we should be able to get a picture of the
name on the side suggested Woolley. The same method was
used to trace the American Submarine Scorpion which sank
in mid Atlantic in 1971. That submarine was lying in
10,000 feet of water.

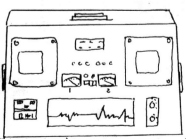

| TV |
| DATA DISPLAY |
| COMPASS DISPLAY |
| TV OPERATION |

FATHAM-LINE TITANIC- Œ-1 REPORT.
ANNEX To APPENDIX III © 986. S 503.

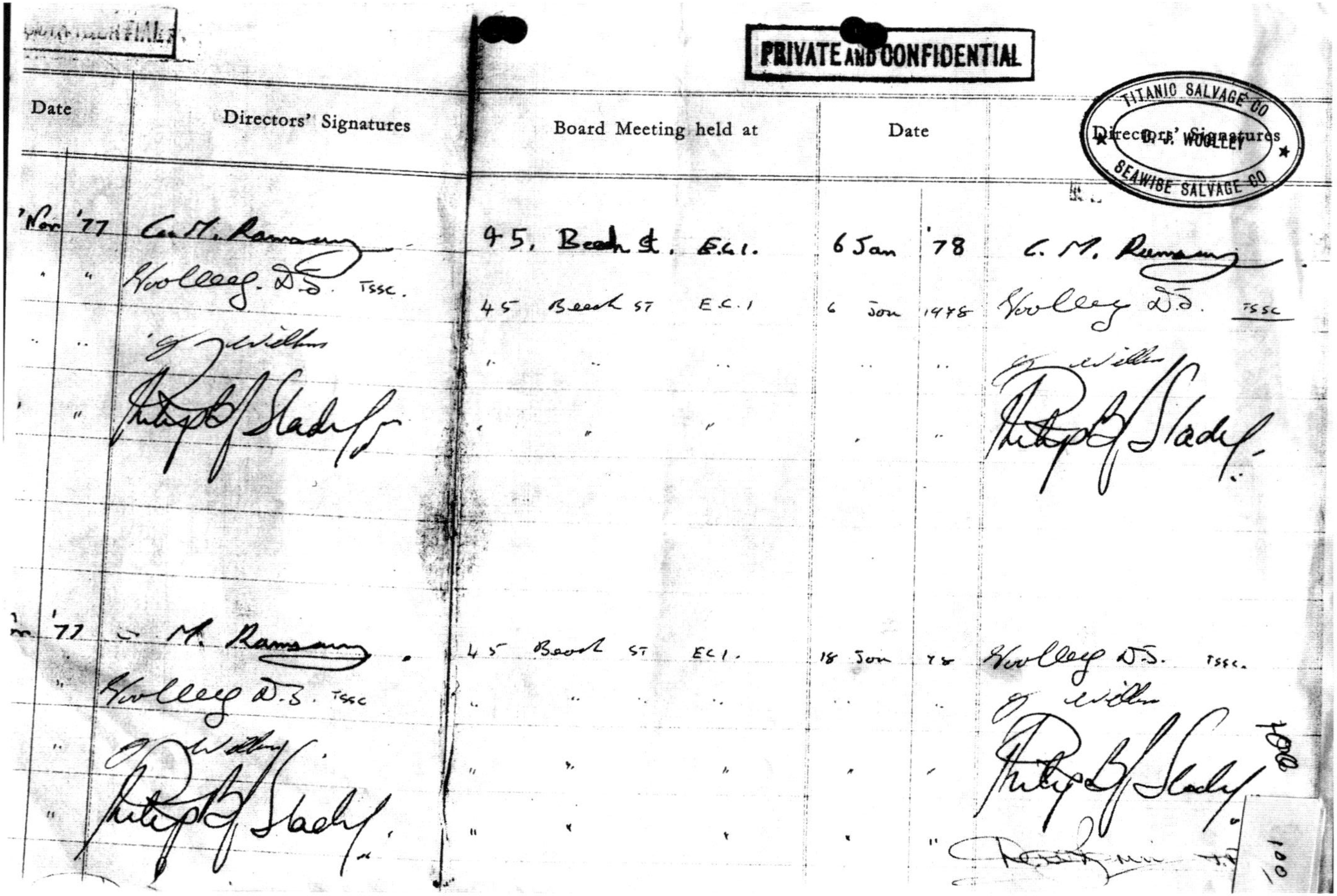

TITANIC SALVAGE CO
SEAWISE SALVAGE CO
Directors' Signatures

Date	Board Meeting held at	Directors' Signatures
6 Jan '78	4·5, Beak St, E.C.I.	C. M. Ramsey _TSSC_
6 Jan 1978	4·5 Beak St E.C.1	Woolley D.S. _TSSC_
"	"	J. Willton
"	"	_(signature)_
18 Jan 78	4·5 Beak St E.C.1.	Woolley D.S. _TSSC_
"	"	J. Willton
"	"	_(signature)_

Date	Board Meeting held at	Directors' Signatures
Nov '77		C. M. Ramsey _TSSC_
"		Woolley D.S. _TSSC_
"		J. Willton
"		_(signature)_
'77		M. Ramsey _TSSC_
"		Woolley D.S. _TSSC_
"		J. Willton
"		_(signature)_

100

70£

SEAWISE AND TITANIC SALVAGE LIMITED

OPENING TRIAL BALANCE

15 APRIL 1988

Nominal Ledger		£	£
1	Ordinary 20p share capital		4,553.00
2	'A' £1 share capital		1,765.00
3	Bank deposit account	307.50	
4	Revenue reserves	5,075.34	
6	Taxation	7.76	
8	Audit and accountancy		675.00
9	Sundry expenses		32.80
13	Dallas Environmental Health shares	492.42	
13A	Dunton Group shares	975.12	
14	Schaverien & Co	42.06	
Cash Book	Cash at bank (current account)	125.60	
		£7,025.80	£7,025.80

SEAWISE SALVAGE CO.
DJW REF. No. 281/162
JERSEY C.I., HONG KONG, U.K.

Douglas Woolley Esq.

TITANIC SALVAGE CO.

E Chase Esq.

11 September 1989.

Dear Elden,

RE: SEAWISE AND TITANIC SALVAGE LTD

    Further to our telephone conversation of today, I confirm that it is unnecessary for you to resign as director of S.T.S. Ltd., as on 28 July 1989, I wrote to companies house applying for the company to be struck off.

    At our last meeting, we agreed to have S.T.S. Ltd. struck off because the company was in such poor condition when the previous directors resigned that it was unable to continue trading. We also agreed that the previous directors had conducted business in such a manner that we felt it wise to close the company before any trading has taken place whilst we were in directorship.

    We further agreed that any business concerning the Queen Elizabeth I or RMS Titanic would be handled by my private company, Titanic Salvage Co. *and Seawise Salvage co. Mr. Stock was Present at the Meeting of SALVORS LD of JERSEY C-I 14 MAY 1972.*

Yours sincerely,

[signature]

DOUGLAS JOHN FAULKNER WOOLLEY
QE1 and TITANIC ... Project
Salvors and ... ... Douglas Woolley
Jersey C.I
U.K. BRITISH HONG KONG

[oval stamp:] TITANIC SALVAGE CO. 102A D.J. WOOLLEY SEAWISE SALVAGE CO.

The QE1 in New York returning with G.I.s on board

The QE1 berthed at Halifax, Nova Scotia

101

THE EPILOGUE

QE1/Seawise salvage costs

Approximately:

Cable	£960,000
Winch	£450,000
35 ml Camera systems	£50,000
Power systems	£30,000
Test equipment	£5,000
Divers each day	£200
Standby safety man per day	£90
Dive masks	£36.60p each
Dive bags for dive equipment	£45.95 each
Flippers	£51.95 per pair
Divers vest & one piece suit	£162
Knives	£42.00
Dive depth gauge	£91.50
TV systems	£65.000
Video recording systems	£20,000
Tool supplies	£20,000

Salvage vessels and tugs not part of this budget plan.

When the money is available a survey will be made, and from that final plans will then be approved. This planning will help to weld the team for the final part of the project - the salvage of the R.M.S. Titanic.

We will need at least three tugs, two tenders and one dive ship and these will allow escort of the QE1 home to the UK.

Those that are to be part of the team must have experience and good capabilities and must agree with and not be afraid of very hard graft. They will be on call 24 hours a day until the QE1 is up and out of Hong Kong and is safe. All wages will be agreed. The budget is only to help plan each stage. The plan will be to run with the Courts in Jersey and Hong Kong and then present the Bill to the Founders of Salvors of Jersey, C.I. and then state why they could not do it in 1972 as agreed. That should have cost only £40,000. This operation will be done in tandem with the Courts.

The Project Stages

1. Planning 1960 to 1971-2
2. Contract - Jersey 1972
3. Royal Court Jersey 1974.
4. Find documents in City of London.
5. Re-open the Court case in Jersey 1988
6. 1994 open Court case in Supreme Court of Hong Kong.
7. a. Operation Poseidon (test)
   b. Operation Flint (QE1)
   c. Operation Hobathy (Titanic)

See no. 6 on assessment of cost:

Assessment of Cost

1. Proven capability.
2. Necessary hardware.
3. In-house expertise.
4. Cost.
5. Timing and time scale.
6. Feasibility and Test.
7. Assessment of team members.
8. Reach conclusion for QE1 and Titanic salvage.

Development costs.	£822,222
Day rate cost and time on survey.	£449,333
Task rate.	£442,666
Total assessed cost of QEI & Titanic survey salvage.	£18,000,000

Operation Poseidon

This operation has been set up to do all the experimental work, tests etc. These will be done by Mr Clive Mead and Mr Richard Bird. They will be based upon the tests done at Shrewsbury and Liverpool in the 1950s and Budapest in 1970/71.

Clive mead has done a reconstruction of the tests that were done in Budapest. These tests were done for the benefit of the authors of the book and for proving the feasibility of the technical data that had been provided.

Doug is still on the look-out for potential team members - do you qualify?

To Those Who Wish To Help

I will try, briefly, to describe to you the responsibilities of my appointments and the assistance and co-operation I will expect from the Directors and members of the public relations and as team members of Seawise and Titanic Salvage.

Public Relations: As its name suggest, Public Relations is to do with the way we present ourselves and our contact with organisation. This means our contact with the press and other media. We are not going to survey the wreck, or indeed raise it, on our own.

We have to attract the attention of organisation with technical expertise and the necessary hardware. How is this going to be possible? the first step we must take is to organise the team. Find who is best

suited to what task. What resources do we have - material and academic? Then we can start to present ourselves as tightly knit, professional and determined group.

Once we are taken seriously, then we have a product we can sell. The probable returns on investment are too incredible to be ignored. If we all work together, and attack the project with enthusiasm, inject it with professionalism, the position of 'Sales Officer' is superfluous, the product will sell itself.

As an administrator, I am going to try and make the above possible. Organise the team, try and bring some order to the chaos that prevails. I cannot do my job without your help. However, each of you are individuals. No single individual will bring this project to its successful conclusion. I am therefore, interested in your performance as a team member. Honesty, in your views and actions, a positive attitude towards the project and team spirit are qualities I am looking for. Do you qualify?

D.J. Faulkner Woolley

WHITE STAR LINE

THE LARGEST STEAMERS IN THE WORLD.

THE LARGEST STEAMERS IN THE WORLD.

"OLYMPIC" (TRIPLE-SCREW) 45,000 TONS.
AND
"TITANIC" (TRIPLE-SCREW) 45,000 TONS.

Close-up of Wychbold Hall, built in the 1830s. Before it was demolished due to subsidence in 1925 children enjoyed playing ball games in the hall because sloping floors. Today, only a keen eye will spot the traces of ballastrades and opening to the cellars.

Wychbold church, the family burial ground for the Amphlett family, as it looked almost 90 years ago

TITANIC.
1912. — *The White Star Line.* — *APPENDIX* — *legal*

The "Titanic" was one of a fleet of thirteen ships employed in the transport of passengers, mails, and cargo between Great Britain and the United States, the usual ports of call for the service in which she was engaged being Southampton, Cherbourg, Plymouth, Queenstown and New York. *Sanderson, 19689-97*

The owners are the Oceanic Steam Navigation Company, Limited, usually known as the White Star Line, a British registered company, with a capital of £750,000, all paid up, the directors being Mr. J. Bruce Ismay (Chairman), the Right *Ismay,* Hon. Lord Pirrie, and Mr. H. A. Sanderson. *18224-69*

The Company are owners of twenty-nine steamers and tenders; they have a large interest in thirteen other steamers, and also own a training sailing ship for officers.

All the shares of the Company, with the exception of eight held by Messrs. E. C. Grenfell, Vivian H. Smith, W. S. M. Burns, James Gray, J. Bruce Ismay, H. A. Sanderson, A. Kerr and the Right Hon. Lord Pirrie, have, since the year 1902, *(ISMAY)* been held by the International Navigation Company, Limited, of Liverpool, a British *PIRIE* registered company, with a capital of £700,000, of which all is paid up, the directors *owl co* being Mr. J. Bruce Ismay (Chairman), and Messrs. H. A. Sanderson, Charles F. Torrey and H. Concanon.

The debentures of the Company, £1,250,000, are held mainly, if not entirely, in the United Kingdom by the general public.

The International Navigation Company, Limited, of Liverpool, in addition *30 July* to holding the above-mentioned shares of the Oceanic Steam Navigation Company, *1912* Limited, is also the owner of :—

  1. Practically the whole of the issued share capital of the British and North Atlantic Steam Navigation Company, Limited, and the Mississippi and Dominion Steamship Company, Limited (the Dominion Line).

  2. Practically the whole of the issued share capital of the Atlantic Transport Company, Limited (the Atlantic Transport Line).

  3. Practically the whole of the issued ordinary share capital and about one-half of the preference share capital of Frederick Leyland and Company, Limited (the Leyland Line).

As against the above-mentioned shares and other property, the International Navigation Company, Limited, have issued share lien certificates for £25,000,000.

Both the shares and share lien certificates of the International Navigation Company, Limited, are now held by the International Mercantile Marine Company of New Jersey, or by trustees for the holders of its debenture bonds.

The Steamship "Titanic."

The "Titanic" was a three-screw vessel of 46,328 tons gross and 21,831 net register tons, built by Messrs. Harland and Wolff for the White Star Line service *Wilding,* between Southampton and New York. She was registered as a British steamship *19789* at the port of Liverpool, her official number being 131,428. Her registered *of reg.* dimensions were :—

Length	852·5 ft.
Breadth	92·5
Depth from top of keel to top of beam at lowest point of sheer of C. Deck, the highest deck which extends continuously from bow to stern	64 ft. 9 in.
Depth of hold	59·58
Height from B to C deck	8·0
„ „ A to B	9·0 „
„ „ Boat to A deck	9·5 „
„ „ Boat deck to waterline amidships at time of accident about	60·5 „
Displacement at 34 ft. 7 in. is	52,310 tons.

123

Capital Letters :- H.V.M.P.

OFFICIAL NUMBER OF SHIP _____ 13/428

Number, Year, and Port of Registry	Number, Year, and Port of previous Registry (if any)	British or Foreign-built
34 / 1913 / Liverpool	New vessel	British

PARTICULARS OF TONNAGE.

		No. of Tons.
GROSS TONNAGE.		
Under Tonnage Deck	...	17870·66
Space or Spaces between Decks ... *below upper middle*		17142·81
Turret or Trunk	...	
Forecastle	...	270·89
Bridge Space	...	3633·45
Poop or Break	...	240·21
Side Houses	...	3904·89
Deck Houses	...	
Chart House	...	
Space for Machinery, Light and Air, s. 78 (2) Merchant Shipping Act, 1894		1,121·16
Excess of Hatchways		
Gross Tonnage ...		46,328·57
Deductions, as per Contra ...		24,497·23
Register Tonnage		21,831·34

DEDUCTIONS ALLOWED.

On account of Space required for Propelling Power ...

On account of Spaces occupied by Seamen or Apprentices, and appropriated to their use, and kept free from Goods or Stores of every kind, not being the personal property of the Crew ...

These Spaces are the following, viz:—
in lower middle after and saloon upper decks
part forecastle bridge and round house

Deductions under s. 79 of the Merchant Shipping Act of 1894, and s. 54 of the Merchant Shipping Act of 1906, as follows:—

	Cubic Metres.
fore peak under & ballast tank	44·43
master accommodation	30·95
engineer stores	16·23
chart room	
	131,109·85
	69,327·16
TOTAL DEDUCTIONS ...	61,423·69

No. of Tons.
21,409·63
24,497
TOTAL DEDUCTIONS ... 24,497

Names, Residence, and Description of the Owners, and Number of Sixty-four Shares held by each Owner ...

Oceanic Steam Navigation Company Limited having its principal place of business at 30 James Street, Liverpool } sixty four Shares

Dated 25th March 1913

Col. 1.	Col. 2.	Col. 3.	Col. 4.	Col. 5.	Col. 6.	Col. 7.	Col. 8.
Number of Transaction.	Date running off Mortgages and Certificates of Mortgage	Name of Person from whom Title is derived.	Number of Shares affected.	Date of Registry	Nature and Date of Transaction.	Name, Residence, and Occupation of Transferee, Mortgagee, or other Person acquiring Title or Power.	Number and Account of subsequent Transaction, showing how Interest disposed of.

106

HANNS ZILCZACK	—	Scotland — Director of Trans-European marketing movements Ltd	none + Reports Consultant marketing movements ltd
JACK F SPARROWS EMANUEL	Noles — This company Monalors investment to Sulphost salvages ↝ Noble a contract to Sulphost Sea Q.E.-1 A Sonars c.ft to Sulphost Sea 1972 and the SALVAGE company R-M-S-...... D.F.E	Czech 67 Souding Street Ataos (40	Quipping Consultant — Note This van Sea company to Sulphost salvage ↝ JP Sonars c.ft Built Monars for Q.E-1 Talcome Sulvage Productt D.F.E Q.C-14/1/D5 F.W.

Date 14/11/72

THE IMPORTANCE OF THE QE1

The QE1 was officially named and launched on 27th September 1938 by Queen Elizabeth, now the Queen Mother.

Just before war broke out the famous Magna Carta was shipped to America for the 1939 New York World's Fair, and afterwards kept in a vault, at the famous Fort Knox in Kentucky, for safety. After the war was over the Magna Carta was returned to England on board the QE1 and that was the most valuable item that was ever carried by this ship, apart from all the troops it carried back and forth during the war years.

When the Second World War started the ship had to be converted for service as a troop transporter. In 1941 America entered into the war and in months that followed she joined her sister ship (Queen Mary), taking American troops to Australia and from there to the Middle East where the desert war was full swing.

Sir Winston Churchill stated that the two Queens had helped to shorten the war in Europe by at least a year and stated: "To those who brought these two great ships into existence, the world owes a debt that will not be easy to measure".

After the war the QE1 was refitted and carried her Cunard colours for the first time. Queen Elizabeth, with her two teenage daughters, went on board during her acceptance trials - 20 years on, one of the daughters would give her own name to the QE2.

The salvage of the QE1 will not be easy and she must be out of Hong Kong as soon as can be, met.
We want to bring her back to England, where she belongs, as part of our history.

The Queen

Douglas John
Faulkner-Woolley

Appendix
Douglas John Faulkner - Woolley
THE NOT SO ORDINARY MAN
QE1 - HONG KONG - SALVAGE

1. PRICE LIST - LIFTING BAGS for the QE1. which can also be used for the Titanic. the price of the lifting bags will be at around £5,500 each, supplied from a company in Holt, norfolk. These will be used for lifting the QE1 in Hong Kong. A lifting frame will be similar to one that was used in lifting The Wellington Bomber on Loch Ness and The Rainbow Warrier from Auckland Harbour. The method being used will be the same as was used when raising The Mary Rose.

2. SURVEY BY JAMES CAMERON. 1995 confirmed my statement of 1960-1972. The fittings of the Titanic are all still there and intact, although people speculated that they would not be there.

3. FAMILY TREE. This has links with the House of Knebworth. They are descendants via MEREDITH A.P. TUDOR. The Tudor line is not only from R. Hon Tagenet and Henry II (Arthur Prince of Wales) and Eleanor of Aquitine, but from the Welsh Kings LLEWELLYN, RHODI MAWR and CADWALLADR. We are a part of his family via the sister of my (Douglas's) great grandmother MARTHA CARTER (Woolley-Finch-Amphlett)

4. The Film TITANIC with Leonardo DiCaprio and Kate Winslet, by James Cameron-Spectacular - but not correct (1998) (Reagent Diamond £120,000,000 on R.M.S TITANIC)

5. The best film to date A NIGHT TO REMEMBER - J. ARTHUR RANK Starring Kenneth More (1958)

6. REPORTS TO SEE - Fathome Report from STS Ltd and now Magazine , 19th October 1979 for the survey of the Titanic.

7. FILM TO SEE - James Bond 007 - The Man With The Golden Gun. (Do not forget it was 1972 NOT 1971)

The End.

DOUG'S
PRESS DIARIES